# Easy And Healthy Dairy-Free Meals For Lazy People

Aedan .Y Major

All rights reserved. Copyright © 2024 Aedan .Y Major

# COPYRIGHT © 2024 Aedan .Y Major

All rights reserved.

No part of this book must be reproduced, stored in a retrieval system, or shared by any means, electronic, mechanical, photocopying, recording, or otherwise, without written permission from the publisher.

Every precaution has been taken in the preparation of this book; still the publisher and author assume no responsibility for errors or omissions. Nor do they assume any liability for damages resulting from the use of the information contained herein.

**Legal Notice:**

This book is copyright protected and is only meant for your individual use. You are not allowed to amend, distribute, sell, use, quote or paraphrase any of its part without the written consent of the author or publisher.

# Introduction

This book is a practical guide designed to facilitate dairy-free cooking for individuals with busy lifestyles. It delves into the nuances of the dairy-free lifestyle, offering insights into why individuals might opt for dairy-free alternatives and the potential benefits associated with such choices. Additionally, it may touch upon the challenges and available substitutes for those transitioning to a dairy-free diet.

Central to the cookbook are its recipes, thoughtfully categorized to accommodate different meal preferences and occasions. These recipes span various categories:

Within the section on Dairy-Free Milks & Cheeses, readers can explore recipes for homemade dairy-free alternatives like almond milk, cashew cheese, or coconut yogurt. This section empowers readers to create nutritious dairy-free options at home.

Smoothies & Breakfasts feature quick and nutrient-rich dairy-free breakfast ideas, including smoothie recipes brimming with fruits, vegetables, and plant-based proteins. These recipes cater to individuals seeking convenient and wholesome breakfast options.

The section on Soups & Salads presents dairy-free soup and salad recipes that are easy to prepare and bursting with flavor. These recipes are ideal for light lunches or dinners, providing nourishing options for health-conscious individuals.

Snacks & Sides offer dairy-free snack ideas and side dishes that complement various meals or serve as standalone treats. These recipes are perfect for satisfying cravings between meals or adding variety to daily eating habits.

Vegetarian Mains feature hearty and satisfying dairy-free main dish recipes centered around vegetables, legumes, grains, and plant-based proteins. These recipes cater to individuals following vegetarian or vegan diets, offering flavorful options for everyday meals.

Meats & Fish provide dairy-free recipes featuring meat and seafood, showcasing a diverse range of flavors and cooking techniques. These recipes offer something for everyone, whether individuals are looking for simple weeknight dinners or impressive dishes for special occasions.

The Desserts section offers dairy-free sweet indulgences, including cakes, cookies, puddings, and fruit-based treats. These recipes cater to individuals with a sweet tooth, ensuring that dairy-free diets do not have to compromise on taste or enjoyment.

Finally, Sauces & Dressings round out the cookbook with dairy-free recipes for enhancing the flavor of meals. From savory sauces to flavorful dressings, these recipes add a finishing touch to dishes without relying on dairy ingredients.

Overall, this book aims to simplify dairy-free cooking and empower individuals to prepare delicious and wholesome meals without sacrificing taste or nutrition. With its diverse range of recipes and emphasis on quick and easy preparation, it serves as a valuable resource for those embracing a dairy-free lifestyle.

# Contents

The Dairy-Free Lifestyle ..................................................................................... 1
Dairy-Free Milks & Cheeses ............................................................................. 19
Cashew Milk ...................................................................................................... 20
Oat Milk ............................................................................................................. 22
Buttermilk .......................................................................................................... 24
Condensed Milk ................................................................................................ 25
Dulce de Leche ................................................................................................. 26
Whipped Cream ................................................................................................ 27
Herbed Goat Cheese ........................................................................................ 28
Grated Parmesan .............................................................................................. 30
Ricotta ............................................................................................................... 31
Cream Cheese .................................................................................................. 33
Sour Cream ....................................................................................................... 34
Butter ................................................................................................................. 35
Smoothies & Breakfasts .................................................................................... 37
Instant Yogurt .................................................................................................... 39
Smooth & Creamy Yogurt ................................................................................. 40
Peanut Butter Split Smoothie ............................................................................ 42
Coffee, Cinnamon & Spice Oats Smoothie ...................................................... 43
Berry-Mango Yogurt Smoothie ......................................................................... 45
Tropical Coconut Yogurt Smoothie Bowl .......................................................... 46
15-Minute Buttermilk Pancakes ........................................................................ 47
Pumpkin Spice Pancakes with Cinnamon Maple Butter .................................. 49
Honey-Oat Griddle Cakes ................................................................................. 51
Peaches & Cream Cheese Pancakes .............................................................. 53
Strawberry Belgian Waffles with Easy Strawberry Syrup ................................ 55
Double Corn Muffins with Chive Butter ............................................................ 57
French Toast Bread Pudding with Maple Caramel .......................................... 59
Caramel-Pecan Sticky Buns ............................................................................. 61
Snickerdoodle Apple Doughnut Muffins ........................................................... 63

Soups & Salads ............................................................................................................... 68
Tomato Alphabet Bisque ................................................................................................ 69
Gingery Carrot & Cashew Bisque ................................................................................. 71
Creamy Corn Soup with Crispy Bacon ......................................................................... 73
Cream of Mushroom Soup ............................................................................................. 75
Basmati Chicken-Ginger Meatball Soup ...................................................................... 77
Avocado Gazpacho ........................................................................................................ 79
Creamy Ranch Summer Pasta Salad ........................................................................... 81
Philly Steak Salad Bowls ............................................................................................... 83
Vietnamese-Style Pork Lettuce Wraps ........................................................................ 84
Shrimp Scampi Caesar Salad ....................................................................................... 86
Warm Roasted Beet, Carrot & Apple Salad with Creamy Poppy Seed Vinaigrette ...... 88
Wedge Salad with Avocado Ranch Dressing & Chickpea Croutons .......................... 90
Snacks & Sides .............................................................................................................. 93
Potato Chips with Caramelized Onion Dip .................................................................. 94
Veggie Crudité with Avocado-Hummus Dip ................................................................ 96
Cream Cheese & Cheddar Stuffed Jalapeño Poppers ................................................ 98
Tortilla Chips with Chipotle Cheese Fondue .............................................................. 100
Double-Baked Sour Cream & Chive Potatoes ........................................................... 101
Three-Cheese Garlic Bread ......................................................................................... 103
Bacon–Brussels Sprouts Hash ................................................................................... 105
Cinnamon-Raisin Bread Breakfast Sausage Stuffing ............................................... 107
Chinese-Style Honey-Mustard Chicken Wings ......................................................... 109
Ranch Chicken Nuggets .............................................................................................. 111
Vegetarian Mains ......................................................................................................... 114
Sicilian Deep-Dish Pizza ............................................................................................. 115
Grilled Vegetable Pizza with Herbed Goat Cheese ................................................... 117
Falafel Taco with Citrus Crema .................................................................................. 119
Veggie Ranchero Bowls .............................................................................................. 121
Stovetop Mac & Cheese .............................................................................................. 123
Eggplant Teriyaki ......................................................................................................... 124
Santa Fe Sweet Potato & Corn Chili .......................................................................... 126
Spaghetti with Creamy Ricotta Pesto Sauce ............................................................. 128

Brussels Sprouts Penne Carbonara ........................................................... 130

Beet-Walnut Veggie Burger with Cheddar Cheese ................................... 132

Sesame Noodles with Broccoli ................................................................. 134

Quinoa Tabbouleh with Smoky Tahini Dressing ....................................... 136

Black Bean–Avocado Burritos .................................................................. 138

Korean Barbecue–Style Veggie Bowl ....................................................... 140

Cauliflower Steaks with Whipped Garlic Ricotta ..................................... 142

Meats & Fish ............................................................................................. 145

Chicken Cordon Bleu with Fondue Dipping Sauce .................................. 146

Skillet Chicken Parmesan ......................................................................... 148

Creamy Chicken-Vegetable Potpie ........................................................... 150

Buffalo Chicken Fingers with Sour Cream & Chive Dip .......................... 152

Sour Cream Mashed Potato–Stuffed Chicken ........................................... 154

Marsala Chicken Pasta Bake ..................................................................... 156

Turkey Sloppy Joe Pizza Pockets ............................................................. 158

Bacon-Wrapped Maple-Mustard Pork Tenderloin .................................... 160

Salsa Steak Tacos ...................................................................................... 162

Boursin-Style Cheese-Stuffed Burgers ..................................................... 164

Tex-Mex Meatloaf Pie ............................................................................... 166

Crispy Fish Sticks with Sweet Relish Tartar Sauce .................................. 168

Fried Shrimp with Creamy Coleslaw ....................................................... 171

Spicy Chipotle Shrimp .............................................................................. 173

Poached Salmon with Dill Pickle Mayo ................................................... 174

Desserts ..................................................................................................... 177

Chocolate Brownie Crinkle Cookies ........................................................ 178

PB&J Cookies ........................................................................................... 180

S'mores Cookie Sandwiches ..................................................................... 182

Dulce de Leche–Stuffed Gingerbread Whoopie Pies ............................... 184

Chocolate-Coconut Magic Bars ............................................................... 186

Chocolate Pudding with Whipped Cream ................................................ 188

Toasted Coconut Snowball Cupcakes ...................................................... 190

Golden Birthday Cupcakes with Chocolate Frosting ............................... 193

Ice Cream Sundae Bonbons ...................................................................... 196

| | |
|---|---|
| Mini Strawberry Shortcakes | 197 |
| Powdered Cake Doughnuts | 199 |
| Fried Cinnamon-Sugar Fritters | 201 |
| Sauces & Dressings | 204 |
| Béchamel | 205 |
| Garlicky Dijon Steak Sauce | 206 |
| Cheese Sauce | 208 |
| Classic Party Fondue | 209 |
| Country Gravy | 211 |
| Egg-Free Mayonnaise | 212 |
| Creamy Poppy Seed Vinaigrette | 213 |
| Ranch Dressing | 214 |
| Caesar Parmesan Dressing | 215 |
| Sour Cream & Chive Dressing | 217 |

# CHAPTER ONE

## The Dairy-Free Lifestyle

Before we get to the recipes, let's talk about what it really means to be dairy-free, how to start on your dairy-free journey, and how to make dairy-free cooking and baking easier than you think. The truth is, when you first go dairy-free, all you can think about are the foods you can't eat anymore, which can be devastating. Once this revelation passes and you start feeling better thanks to eliminating dairy from your diet, a shift happens—and so does your openness to cooking and baking again. In this chapter, I've outlined what it means to be dairy-free and answered the most common questions about the dairy-free diet, along with tips on how to make the transition easier.

# WHY DAIRY-FREE?

Why go dairy-free? There are plenty of reasons why people explore the benefits of a dairy-free diet. Maybe you're allergic, intolerant, or need to improve your overall health. Or maybe you want improved digestion and nutrition absorption or clearer skin. I'm still amazed that by making changes in our diet, we have the power to help our bodies thrive.

Allergies, intolerances, and sensitivities are very real, and your health must be your top priority. Eliminating dairy may seem scary at first, but it helps knowing you can get the calcium you need from many other sources and that you don't have to miss out on foods you love; you just have to adapt them a little.

# MILK ALLERGY

Milk is a surprisingly common food allergy, especially in young children. There are about 4.5 million people in the United States who are allergic to milk. A milk allergy results in a heightened response by the immune system to the casein and whey proteins found in milk. Casein is the curd that forms when milk sours, and whey is the watery by-product left behind after the curd is removed.

Allergic reactions triggered when you ingest milk proteins can range from mild symptoms, including rashes and bloating, to severe symptoms like vomiting, wheezing, and shortness of breath.

So, how do you know if you have a milk allergy? While there are clinical allergy tests available, many doctors now recommend a simple elimination diet to easily identify whether or not your body has an adverse response to milk. An elimination diet first removes milk (or other foods) from your diet for four to six weeks, then slowly reintroduces the foods one at a time to see if your body reacts negatively and the symptoms return. If milk is indeed the reason for your symptoms, the only known treatment is to avoid milk completely. Instead of using milk, go ahead and swap in dairy-free ingredients as simple substitutions.

## LACTOSE INTOLERANCE

Lactose intolerance is the inability to break down a type of natural sugar called lactose. According to the National Institute of Diabetes and Digestive and Kidney Diseases, one in six people in the United States are lactose intolerant. You become lactose intolerant when your small intestine stops making enough of the enzyme lactase to digest and break down lactose, which causes symptoms such as bloating, gas, abdominal cramps, nausea, and diarrhea.

If you experience any of these symptoms after eating dairy, you can take a blood or stool test to confirm whether you are lactose intolerant. It is important to remember that if you're lactose intolerant, it means you can't eat any form of dairy, not just milk, as with a milk allergy.

While there are over-the-counter lactase enzyme supplements available at the drugstore you can take before eating dairy products, and some lactose-free products are available at the supermarket, the best treatment for long-term health is to cut dairy completely out of your diet.

## FOOD SENSITIVITY

A dairy sensitivity or intolerance is different from a milk allergy or lactose intolerance. Unlike an allergy, where you tend to have symptoms immediately after eating the offending foods, a sensitivity often has delayed reactions. Food allergies trigger your immune system. A sensitivity usually means your body simply has difficulty digesting those foods and is not the histamine/immune response of an allergy. If you have a negative reaction when you eat dairy, including headaches, stomachaches, bloating, acne, or hives, your body is trying to tell you something. Since about 80 percent of the immune system is in the gut, anything that upsets your digestion could disrupt other systems in your body.

Keep track of which types of dairy might be troubling you. Maybe your body tolerates goat's milk or sheep's milk but isn't a fan of cow's milk. To determine if you have a dairy sensitivity, start an elimination diet and go without dairy for at least 30 days. Keep a journal and take notes of any improved health effects, the disappearance of any symptoms, and whether you have more energy or are sleeping better. Then, slowly reintroduce dairy into your diet and see how your body responds.

## GENERAL HEALTH BENEFITS

If you don't have a milk allergy or intolerance and decide to ditch dairy for general health reasons, you may still see changes in your body. Some of the health benefits associated with a dairy-free lifestyle include clearer skin, more consistent digestion, lower amounts of inflammation and bloating, and lower insulin levels. Eliminating dairy can even lead to weight loss for some people.

Acne and other skin conditions are often inflammatory conditions, and the proteins in dairy products are known to increase inflammation not just in your skin, but in your intestines and glands, as well. Inflammation can cause headaches, joint pain, and bloating, too. Dairy is also mucus-producing, so giving it up can potentially improve your metabolism and lead to weight loss. Many people who have cut dairy from their diet have experienced clearer skin and less bloating and gas. While dairy alone is not scientifically linked to skin conditions, many doctors and nutritionists recommend elimination diets to see if cutting it out helps resolve the problem.

# UNDERSTANDING FOOD LABELS

It may seem obvious what foods contain dairy—cow's milk, buttermilk, butter, cheese, ice cream, and yogurt—and what foods don't. The reality is that packaged and processed foods like deli meats, salad dressings, granola bars, hot dogs, potato chips, and even spice mixes sometimes contain dairy. Food labels can be confusing, especially when you're new to shopping for dairy-free items. Here are a few tips for looking at labels when buying packaged and processed foods:

## NONDAIRY

Contrary to popular belief, "nondairy" does not actually mean milk-free. The FDA regulatory definition for "nondairy" actually allows a product labeled as such to contain up to 0.5 percent milk protein by weight. The regulation allows for the presence of milk protein, such as casein, whey, and other dairy derivatives. Casein is the main protein found in milk and cheese, while whey, which is often used in protein powders, is the liquid part of milk that remains once it has been curdled and strained. In these foods, the FDA says the label must include "caseinate" in the ingredients list and include what kind of caseinate it is, such as "milk derivative."

Carefully reading nutrition labels becomes critical, especially if you have a dairy allergy or your dairy intolerance is severe. Some popular hidden ingredients that contain dairy include artificial or natural flavors, lactic acid starter culture, and prebiotics.

## DAIRY-FREE

There is no FDA regulatory definition for "dairy-free," but this label is a better indicator of whether a food is actually free of dairy. Better yet, thanks to the Food Allergen Labeling and Consumer Protection Act, food manufacturers are required to declare the eight top allergens, including dairy, on their labeling. Look for the disclaimer below the ingredient list that states which allergen a product contains.

Another label to look for is "vegan," which, based on dietary guidelines, means the product will be dairy-free. That said, if you have a severe allergy, it's best to contact the manufacturer directly. Some foods could be dairy-free themselves but are produced in a facility that also processes dairy, which could still negatively affect someone with an allergy or severe intolerance.

## KOSHER

The Hebrew word "kosher" indicates that a food is "fit and proper" as it relates to Jewish dietary law and commonly refers to foods which are either all dairy with no meat in them or all meat with no dairy. In addition to the kosher label, foods marked with a "parev"/"pareve" designation means they have been prepared without milk, meat, or their derivatives and are "neutral" in the Jewish diet. Pareve food examples include fruits, grains, margarine, vegetables, and eggs. However, people with severe allergies should note that just because there is no dairy or meat in the product itself, the product may have been made on a machine or in the same room as other foods with dairy or meat in them. This means there is the potential of cross-contamination, which is likely only a concern if you have a severe dairy allergy. Again, to be sure, contact the manufacturer directly.

# THE CALCIUM CONUNDRUM

People transitioning to a dairy-free diet often wonder or are asked how they plan to get calcium. The truth is that milk isn't the only food or drink with calcium. How much calcium you need depends on your gender, age, and level of physical activity, but according to the National Osteoporosis Foundation, in general, women under age 50 need 1000 mg daily, while women over age 51 need 1200 mg. Men under 70 need about 1000 mg and men over 70 need about 1200 mg. Calcium is very important for bone development and for other functions, such as maintaining your teeth, blood clotting, transmission of nerve impulses, and regulating your heartbeat. The reason it's necessary to ingest calcium from the foods we eat is because most of our body's calcium is stored in our bones and teeth. When we don't eat enough of it, our body "borrows" the calcium from our bones with the intention that it will be replaced through eating calcium-rich foods. If that calcium isn't replaced, bones become porous and this leads to osteoporosis.

There are many foods to get calcium from other than milk, including cabbage, broccoli, edamame and other soy products, tahini, almonds, shrimp, salmon, and dried fruit, such as raisins and apricots. Other calcium-rich foods that are dairy-free include most dark, leafy greens like collard greens, spinach, and kale; seeds, such as poppy seeds, sesame seeds, celery seeds, and chia seeds; sardines, beans, lentils, rhubarb, tofu, and figs. There are also quite a few calcium-fortified drinks on the market.

In this cookbook, you'll find calcium-rich recipes such as [Poached Salmon with Dill Pickle Mayo](), [Fried Shrimp with Creamy Coleslaw](), [Veggie Crudité with Avocado-Hummus Dip](), and [Quinoa Tabbouleh with Smoky Tahini Dressing](). Since our bodies use calcium throughout the day, we need to replace it through our diet. While food is the best source for calcium, with a better nutritional absorption rate, some doctors and nutritionists also recommend taking calcium supplements with or without vitamin D, which helps your body absorb calcium and use it properly.

# THE DAIRY-FREE KITCHEN: TIPS FOR EASIER COOKING

Want to make the dairy-free transition even easier? There are a few tools and ingredients that benefit a dairy-free kitchen specifically, particularly if you're trying to make dairy-free recipes quickly. You must be open to breaking traditional culinary rules and trying new-to-you ingredients to re-create the specific textures of dairy-based ingredients, which is critical for recipe outcome and visual appeal.

Let's jump in and see how you can supplement your kitchen to create the perfect dairy-free cooking environment.

## HIGH-SPEED BLENDER

Simply put, high-speed blenders are more powerful than the average blender. With motors that have more horsepower and performance-designed blades, there's no question you will get a better outcome. Texture is everything, especially when you're making dairy-free versions of base ingredients, like milk, yogurt, or goat cheese. You'll also save time, because you won't need a sieve to strain out the little pieces of ingredients that aren't processed enough by average blenders.

## FOOD PROCESSOR

At first glance, a food processor and blender seem to perform similar tasks. In some cases, they can be interchangeable. The main differences are in the blades and what they are used for. Unlike a blender's blades, the blades of a food processor are razor-sharp, and food processors often come with additional attachments or blades for slicing, shredding, chopping, and mixing dough. Food processors also usually have larger components, making it easier to make bigger batches and to add ingredients during processing. Overall, blenders are better for liquids, and food processors are great for more labor-intensive things like grinding nuts and making butters. I tend to use a food processor to process drier recipes like grated Parmesan and the blender to make smoother, more liquid-based recipes like milk and yogurt.

## IMMERSION BLENDER

This is all you need to transform a soup or sauce from chunky to smooth and creamy—and it takes up less space than a regular blender or food processor. Immersion blenders are handheld and sometimes referred to as "stick blenders." Because they are so much smaller and have fewer parts, they are easier to clean, and some cooks prefer to use an immersion blender over a regular one.

## AUTOMATIC YOGURT MAKER

This inexpensive small appliance will deliver a wonderfully rich and creamy yogurt safely. You can even decide how thick you prefer the yogurt, then set the optimal cooking time and temperature so good bacteria will grow and live active cultures will thrive. Despite the name, these machines are not fully automatic. You'll need to spend 15 to 30 minutes preparing the milk by heating it and then cooling it before adding it to the yogurt maker with the starter culture for the beneficial bacteria.

## NUT MILK BAG

You can use this reusable superfine mesh bag with a drawstring to strain solids from liquids, which is necessary for nut-based milks and cheeses if you aren't using a high-speed blender. You can also use a nut milk bag in place of cheesecloth to thicken the consistency of yogurt or cheese. Use the drawstring to hang the bag, then set over a large bowl to strain. This is a very useful and inexpensive tool.

## CHEESECLOTH OR MUSLIN FABRIC

Cheesecloth is inexpensive and versatile. I often use it to strain liquids out of various milk and cheese recipes. You can find packages of precut cheesecloth in most large supermarkets or purchase inexpensive plain muslin cloth at a fabric store and cut it to the size you need. Make sure the muslin is 100 percent cotton and unbleached, and wash before using it for cooking. The benefit of muslin is that it is reusable, unlike cheesecloth, but performs the same functions for draining liquids.

## 12-INCH BALLOON WHISK

The most important task a whisk performs in my kitchen is aeration. In my experience, this large whisk performs better than a flour sifter or sieve. Instead of using a wooden spoon or silicone spatula, I often use a whisk to aerate pancake and cupcake batters, which makes them lighter in texture.

# DAIRY & MILK ALTERNATIVES

Milk and general dairy alternatives are important in your dairy-free lifestyle, and there are many to choose from. Listed below are the dairy-free ingredients I use most in my kitchen either as a key ingredient in creating dairy-free base recipes like milk, yogurt, and cheese or as an ingredient in general recipes. Each one has different uses and textures, and it's fun to experiment and see what you like best and why.

## CASHEW MILK

Cashew milk is the most neutral-tasting homemade milk, which is why I use it in many of the recipes in this cookbook. Because of the high fat content of cashews, this milk is ultra-creamy in texture.

## OAT MILK

Oat milk is also neutral in flavor and naturally slightly sweet. If I buy dairy-free milk in the supermarket, it's always refrigerated unsweetened oat milk. You can also buy sweetened oat milk, which is great for smoothies, cereal, and cappuccinos.

## FULL-FAT COCONUT MILK

I use the solid cream spooned off the top of a refrigerated can of full-fat coconut milk to make luscious and airy whipped cream for desserts. Coconut milk is also great in curries and other recipes.

## YOUNG COCONUT MEAT

This meat comes from a green coconut and is the soft, fleshy part of a mature brown coconut. It naturally contains living enzymes, which help with digestion and metabolism. It's great for creating silky textures, especially in yogurt and smoothies. Young coconut meat can be found in the freezer section of many health food stores and you can order it online.

## NUTRITIONAL YEAST

This fiber-packed inactive yeast is used in dairy-free cooking as an umami-rich seasoning and delivers a cheesy, nutty flavor. I use it to make cheese sauces and Parmesan. Nutritional yeast is vegan and highly nutritious.

## NONHYDROGENATED SHORTENING

I often prefer to use this vegetable-based fat in baked goods to replace dairy-based unsalted butter. It can be substituted in a 1:1 ratio.

# DAIRY-FREE YOGURT CULTURE STARTER

This blend of lactic acid bacteria helps culture dairy-free milk to make yogurt, yielding a characteristically mild sourness with a smooth, creamy texture. It's an essential ingredient in dairy-free yogurt and is added right to your milk before being placed in the automatic yogurt maker.

# PROBIOTIC POWDER

This powder contains healthy, live bacteria and enzymes that not only make food more digestible but also add a slightly tangy and sour flavor. In dairy-free yogurt and cheese–making, probiotic powder is the key ingredient that delivers the quintessential tang reminiscent of dairy products. You can also add probiotic powder to smoothies and other recipes for additional help with digestion.

# SUNFLOWER LECITHIN

Lecithin is a substance naturally found in the tissues of your body and is made of fatty acids. Lecithin can be derived from sunflower seeds, eggs, or soybeans, and works as an emulsifier in cooking. I use sunflower lecithin, which is high in antioxidants. Lecithin makes foods extra creamy and rich—which is why I use it in my [Butter](Butter).

# DATE SYRUP

This neutral-flavored, sweet, quick-dissolving syrup is made from Medjool dates. When making some of the dairy-free basics, like milk or yogurt, I like to use just a touch of sweetener to mimic the natural lactose sugars found in milk. It can also be used as a sweetener in any number of recipes.

# NEUTRAL-FLAVORED OILS

In some recipes, especially the dairy-free basic recipes in which I use oil as an emulsifier—not for flavor—I prefer neutral-flavored oils. I have avocado oil in my kitchen, but you could use whatever you have on hand, such as sunflower oil, grapeseed oil, or even a blended vegetable oil. These oils are found in most large supermarkets.

# WHAT ABOUT EGGS?

Typically, an allergy or intolerance to milk doesn't impact your ability to eat eggs. Despite being sold in the dairy aisle, eggs are naturally dairy-free. According to the USDA, dairy is defined as "all fluid milk products and foods made from milk." In fact, eggs are considered animal products and belong to the meat, poultry, fish, and eggs category.

That said, people who have a dairy allergy may also be allergic to one or more of the other top eight allergens, including eggs. Since this is a dairy-free cookbook, I've included recipes with eggs—however, I have also given options for egg substitutes (see here). Keep in mind that eggs provide structure, stability, leavening, thickening, emulsifying, color, and flavor, especially to baked goods. While my egg alternatives mimic real eggs, they don't have all the same properties, and the resulting textures may not be identical.

If you're using an egg substitute in a baking recipe, increase baking time by about 5 minutes.

## ABOUT THE RECIPES

Most of the recipes in this cookbook are designed to take 30 minutes or less. Some recipes may include ingredients that can be easily made separately and ahead of time (like dairy-free milk, butter, or cheese) and stored until you are ready to cook. The recipes in chapter 2 are foundational. Some may take over 30 minutes to complete but are important to include and can be made ahead of time and stored. If you're short on time, you can certainly purchase these ingredients at your local supermarket or health food store. I've noted this in the recipe ingredient lists throughout the cookbook.

## LABELS THAT INDICATE EASE

You already know that the recipes in this book can be made in under 30 minutes, but many of these recipes fall into categories that highlight further how easy they are. The categories include One-Pot,

5-Ingredient, Make-Ahead, and Good for Leftovers. All recipes will be labeled with their corresponding attributes.

# TIPS THAT MAKE THINGS EVEN EASIER

Most of the recipes in this book also include a recipe tip, such as a substitution tip when an ingredient can be swapped out for flavor or allergy reasons; a time-saving swap, like using a store-bought ingredient in place of making it yourself; or a cooking tip to make the recipe easier to prep or to give alternative cooking methods.

# DIETARY LABELS

You'll note that I use the following dietary labels for each recipe as they fit the category: Egg-Free, Gluten-Free, Nut-Free, Vegan, and Vegetarian. For recipes that include eggs, I've also included egg substitute options so you can make the choice about which to use. These labels let you know at a glance what will work for you and your dietary needs.

**Dulce de Leche**

# CHAPTER TWO

# Dairy-Free Milks & Cheeses

Cashew Milk

Oat Milk

Buttermilk

Condensed Milk

Dulce de Leche

Whipped Cream

Herbed Goat Cheese

Grated Parmesan

Ricotta

Cream Cheese

Sour Cream

Butter

# Cashew Milk

5-INGREDIENT, EGG-FREE, GLUTEN-FREE, MAKE-AHEAD, VEGAN
MAKES 4 CUPS / PREP TIME: 5 MINUTES, PLUS 4 HOURS TO SOAK

This is the most versatile nut milk, and, because of the high fat content of cashews, it has an incredibly creamy texture. If you prefer your milk unsweetened, leave out the date syrup or dates in the recipe. I prefer adding a spoonful of date syrup for its caramel-like flavor and because it's high in antioxidants, potassium, and magnesium. You can go ahead and swap in what you have in your pantry, including maple syrup, agave syrup, or even honey. No time to soak the cashews? Use a heaping ¼ cup of cashew butter instead of raw cashews.

**1 cup raw cashews, soaked for at least 4 hours or overnight, rinsed and drained**

**1 to 2 tablespoons date syrup or 1 to 2 pitted dates (optional)**

**Seeds of 1 vanilla bean or 2 teaspoons pure vanilla extract (optional)**

**¼ teaspoon salt**

**4 cups water**

1. Add the cashews, date syrup or dates (if using), vanilla (if using), salt, and water to a high-speed blender and process on high speed until smooth, about 1 minute.

2. Pour through a coarse-mesh sieve over a medium bowl to strain.

3. Store in a resealable container in the refrigerator for up to 1 week.

Ingredient Tip: To make nonfat milk, use 5 cups of water. For low-fat milk, use 4 cups of water. For whole-fat milk, use 3 cups of water. To make heavy cream or creamer, use 2 to 2½ cups water plus 1 tablespoon of neutral-flavored oil for extra creaminess.

# Oat Milk

**5-INGREDIENT, EGG-FREE, MAKE-AHEAD, VEGAN**
**MAKES 4 CUPS / PREP TIME: 5 MINUTES, PLUS 15 MINUTES TO SOAK**

There's a reason oat milk is usually sold out at the supermarket—it's neutral in flavor and has a wonderful viscosity, which you get by blending the milk with your favorite oil. Adding oil makes it froth well for your morning cappuccino. For sweetener, I love using date syrup, but any sweetener will do. Add your favorite to get the flavor you love. Check out the tips below to get different flavored milks after making your neutral oat milk.

**1 cup old-fashioned steel-cut oats, soaked for 15 minutes, rinsed well and drained**

**1 to 2 tablespoons date syrup or 1 to 2 pitted dates (optional)**

**Seeds of 1 vanilla bean or 2 teaspoons pure vanilla extract (optional)**

**1 tablespoon neutral-flavored oil**

**¼ teaspoon salt**

**4 cups water**

1. Add the oats, date syrup (if using), vanilla (if using), oil, salt, and up to 4 cups water to a high-speed blender and process on high speed until smooth, about 1 minute.

2. Pour through a coarse-mesh sieve over a medium bowl to strain.

3. Store in a resealable container in the refrigerator for up to 1 week.

Substitution Tips:

**CHOCOLATE MILK:** Add 1 tablespoon cocoa powder to 1 cup strained oat milk and blend to combine.

**STRAWBERRY MILK:** Add ½ cup hulled fresh or frozen strawberries to 1 cup strained milk and blend to combine.

**PUMPKIN SPICE MILK:** Add ½ teaspoon pumpkin pie spice and ¼ teaspoon pure vanilla extract.

**MATCHA MILK:** Add 1 tablespoon matcha green tea powder.

**GOLDEN MILK:** Add 2 teaspoons ground turmeric, ½ teaspoon ground cinnamon, ¼ teaspoon ground cardamom, and ⅛ teaspoon black pepper and mix well.

# Buttermilk

**5-INGREDIENT, EGG-FREE, MAKE-AHEAD, VEGAN**
**MAKES 2 CUPS / PREP TIME: 10 MINUTES**

Not only does buttermilk give a recipe its quintessential tang, it also gives textures a lift. In this recipe, the acidity from the vinegar will give your baked goods that same boost and tang. This version doesn't have buttermilk's thick viscosity, which I found isn't necessary for optimal recipe performance. If you want a thicker consistency, you can blend in xanthan gum, a pinch at a time, until you reach your desired consistency; this will not affect flavor. The buttermilk will keep refrigerated in a resealable container for up to 3 days.

**2 cups homemade Oat Milk or store-bought dairy-free oat milk**

**2 tablespoons apple cider vinegar**

In a small bowl, whisk together the milk and vinegar. Let stand until the mixture begins to slightly curdle, about 10 minutes. Use immediately or refrigerate for up to 3 days.

Substitution Tip: You can use lemon juice or distilled white vinegar in place of the apple cider vinegar.

# Condensed Milk

5-INGREDIENT, EGG-FREE, GLUTEN-FREE, MAKE-AHEAD, VEGAN
MAKES 1½ CUPS / PREP TIME: 4 MINUTES / COOK TIME: 1 HOUR 30 MINUTES

Confession: I developed this recipe as my gateway to Dulce de Leche. You can substitute this blend cup for cup in any recipe that calls for traditional condensed milk. The milk will keep refrigerated in a resealable container for up to 2 weeks. If it thickens too much, whisk in some water, 1 teaspoon at a time, to get your desired consistency.

**4 cups homemade Cashew Milk or store-bought dairy-free cashew milk**

**1¾ cups sugar**

1. In a small saucepan over medium heat, bring the milk and sugar to a boil.
2. Reduce the heat and simmer, stirring occasionally to prevent a skin from forming, until reduced by about half and thickened, about 1 hour and 30 minutes.
3. Remove from the heat and cover the surface directly with plastic wrap. Let cool completely before storing in an airtight container.

# Dulce de Leche

5-INGREDIENT, EGG-FREE, GLUTEN-FREE, MAKE-AHEAD, VEGAN
MAKES 1½ CUPS / PREP TIME: 3 MINUTES / COOK TIME: 40 MINUTES

A slow-cooked caramel sauce made of sweetened milk; I cook this intensely caramel-like spread in tight-seal lidded glass jars in my slow cooker, but you can make it on the stovetop, as seen here. I love spreading dulce de leche on toast or drizzling it over ice cream, yogurt, and pancakes. The dulce de leche will keep refrigerated for up to 2 weeks.

**2 cups homemade <u>Condensed Milk</u> or store-bought dairy-free condensed milk**

**Pinch salt**

1. Combine the condensed milk and pinch salt in a double boiler or a heatproof bowl set over a saucepan of boiling water.
2. Cover tightly with a lid or foil and cook over low heat, stirring occasionally, until thickened and light caramel in color, about 40 minutes.
3. Remove from heat and beat until smooth.

Cooking Tip: To make this dulce de leche in a slow cooker, combine the condensed milk and salt in heatproof glass jars and seal the lids tightly. Pour water in the slow cooker to completely cover the jars by about an inch. Cover and cook on low for 8 to 10 hours, then remove the jars carefully and let them come down to room temperature before storing in the refrigerator.

# Whipped Cream

5-INGREDIENT, EGG-FREE, GLUTEN-FREE, MAKE-AHEAD
MAKES 1¼ CUPS / PREP TIME: 5 MINUTES

This luscious, billowy whipped cream is made with the cream spooned off the top of a refrigerated can of high-fat coconut milk. Depending on the brand you use, the amount of coconut cream you get from one can does vary; I've gotten from half a can to almost the entire can of cream. If you regularly get half, use 2 cans of coconut milk. What makes it light and airy is the tiny bit of water whipped in at the end. For best results, stick the mixing bowl and electric beaters in the freezer before you start whipping. This whipped cream can be refrigerated in a resealable container for up to 1 week.

**1 (13-ounce) can full-fat coconut milk, refrigerated overnight**

**2 tablespoons confectioners' sugar**

**⅛ teaspoon salt**

**1 teaspoon water**

1. Spoon the solid coconut cream from the top of the coconut milk into a medium bowl.
2. With an electric mixer, whip the cream together with the confectioners' sugar on medium-high speed until stiff peaks begin to form.
3. Whip in the salt and water.

Substitution Tip: You can make this whipped cream even lighter by whipping in up to ½ cup of store-bought marshmallow cream for every 1 cup coconut cream.

# Herbed Goat Cheese

**EGG-FREE, GLUTEN-FREE, MAKE-AHEAD, VEGAN**
MAKES 4 TO 6 SERVINGS / PREP TIME: 8 MINUTES, PLUS 8 HOURS TO DRAIN AND 8 HOURS TO SET

This make-ahead recipe is great for entertaining or even a late-night snack. Probiotics give this cheese a nice tang reminiscent of its goat's milk–based counterpart. The goat cheese will keep refrigerated in a resealable container for up to 1 week.

**1 cup raw macadamia nuts, soaked for at least 4 hours or overnight, rinsed and drained**

**1 cup raw cashews, soaked for at least 4 hours or overnight, rinsed and drained**

**1¼ teaspoons salt (1 teaspoon used first, then ¼ teaspoon used later)**

**2 teaspoons lemon juice**

**1 teaspoon dairy-free probiotic powder**

**½ cup water**

**⅓ cup finely chopped fresh mixed herbs, such as rosemary, parsley, and thyme**

**1 tablespoon lemon zest**

**½ teaspoon coarsely cracked pepper**

1. Blend together the macadamia nuts, cashews, 1 teaspoon of salt, lemon juice, probiotic powder, and ½ cup water in a high-speed blender until smooth.
2. Place the mixture in a damp cheesecloth-lined strainer set over a bowl and fold the sides of the cheesecloth to loosely cover.
3. Top with a weight and let drain at room temperature for at least

8 hours or overnight.

4. To form a log, place the cheese in the middle of a large piece of plastic wrap and roll up, twisting the ends. Refrigerate until set, at least 8 hours.

5. After the cheese log is set, in a small bowl, stir together the chopped herbs, lemon zest, pepper, and remaining ¼ teaspoon of salt. Roll the cheese log in the herb mixture to coat completely and serve.

---

Cooking Tip: To create a weight, I like to use 1 or 2 cans of beans, but any heavy kitchen item will do.

# Grated Parmesan

5-INGREDIENT, EGG-FREE, GLUTEN-FREE, MAKE-AHEAD, VEGAN
MAKES 1 CUP / PREP TIME: 1 MINUTE

This speedy recipe gets faux-Parmesan cheese on your table in just minutes. The secret is nutritional yeast, a fiber-packed inactive yeast you can find in your local health food store that delivers a cheesy flavor. The Parmesan will keep in a resealable container for up to 1 week.

**¾ cup raw macadamia nuts**

**¼ cup nutritional yeast**

**½ teaspoon salt**

Using a food processor or a blender, pulse together the macadamia nuts, nutritional yeast, and salt. Refrigerate for up to 1 week.

Ingredient Tip: Nutritional yeast has a nutty cheesy flavor and, like Parmesan, is a great topper for popcorn, pasta, vegetables, and salads. Add it on top of your favorite recipes for additional deliciousness.

# Ricotta

EGG-FREE, GLUTEN-FREE, MAKE-AHEAD, VEGAN
MAKES 2 CUPS / PREP TIME: 5 MINUTES, PLUS OVERNIGHT TO SOAK

Pine nuts remind you of ricotta's Italian origins while macadamia nuts give this cheese extra creaminess. A touch of date syrup replaces the lactose sugar found in cow's milk. This dairy-free ricotta alternative is great for pasta recipes.

**1 cup raw pine nuts, soaked for at least 4 hours or overnight, rinsed and drained**

**1 cup raw macadamia nuts, soaked for at least 4 hours or overnight, rinsed and drained**

**2 tablespoons olive oil**

**1 tablespoon lemon juice**

**½ teaspoon date syrup**

**1 teaspoon salt**

**¼ cup plus 1 tablespoon water (used all at once)**

1. Add the pine nuts, macadamia nuts, oil, lemon juice, date syrup, and salt to a food processor and pulse to combine.

2. While the food processor is still running, slowly stream in ¼ cup plus 1 tablespoon water and continue mixing, scraping down the sides of the bowl if necessary, until light and fluffy, about 3 minutes.

3. Use immediately or refrigerate in a resealable container for up to 1 week.

**Substitution Tip:** To make a sweet ricotta, which is great for filling cannoli shells or spreading on toast, swap in neutral-tasting avocado oil for the olive oil, add 3 tablespoons sugar, 1 teaspoon pure vanilla extract, and the zest of 1 orange or other citrus.

# **Cream Cheese**

EGG-FREE, GLUTEN-FREE, MAKE-AHEAD, VEGAN
MAKES 1 CUP / PREP TIME: 5 MINUTES, PLUS 1 HOUR TO SET

What would a world of bagels without cream cheese be? I didn't want to know, so I developed this tangy, dairy-free cream cheese that's thick and spreadable just like the real deal. The cream cheese will keep refrigerated in a resealable container for up to 1 week.

**½ cup raw macadamia nuts, soaked for at least 4 hours or overnight, rinsed and drained**

**½ cup raw cashews, soaked for at least 4 hours or overnight, rinsed and drained**

**½ teaspoon dairy-free probiotic powder**

**¼ cup refined coconut oil**

**½ teaspoon date syrup**

**¼ teaspoon salt**

1. Add the macadamia nuts, cashews, probiotic powder, oil, date syrup, and salt to a high-speed blender and process on high speed until smooth.

2. Place the mixture in a damp cheesecloth-lined strainer set over a bowl and fold the sides of the cheesecloth to loosely cover.

3. Refrigerate for at least 1 hour or overnight to set.

Ingredient Tip: Flavor your cream cheese by stirring in chopped scallions, chopped sun-dried tomatoes, soaked and drained raisins, or chopped walnuts.

# Sour Cream

**EGG-FREE, GLUTEN-FREE, MAKE-AHEAD, VEGAN**
**MAKES 1 CUP / PREP TIME: 6 MINUTES, PLUS 1 HOUR FOR THICKENING**

I've added several layers of acidity to get the perfect sourness in this recipe, including lemon juice, vinegar, and a dairy-free probiotic powder to mimic tartness. You can use this sour cream in both sweet and savory recipes. The more time you soak the nuts, the smoother the consistency will be. This sour cream will keep refrigerated in a resealable container for up to 1 week.

**1 cup raw cashews, soaked for at least 4 hours or overnight, rinsed and drained**

**3 tablespoons lemon juice**

**1 teaspoon distilled white vinegar**

**1 teaspoon gluten-free chickpea miso**

**¾ teaspoon salt**

**½ teaspoon dairy-free probiotic powder**

**¾ cup water**

Add the cashews, lemon juice, vinegar, miso, salt, probiotic powder, and water to a high-speed blender and process on high speed until smooth. Refrigerate until cold and thickened, about 1 hour.

# Butter

EGG-FREE, GLUTEN-FREE, MAKE-AHEAD, VEGAN
MAKES 1 CUP / PREP TIME: 5 MINUTES, PLUS 30 MINUTES FOR FREEZING

It means everything to be able to spread butter on bread, put a pat of butter on potatoes, and of course, use butter in your cooking and baking. For this recipe, I like to use cacao butter, which is the cold-pressed oil of a cacao bean and a healthy source of antioxidants and omega-6 and omega-9 fatty acids. This butter will keep refrigerated for up to 1 month.

**¼ cup refined coconut oil, melted**

**2 tablespoons raw cacao butter, preferably flavorless, melted**

**1 tablespoon neutral-flavored oil**

**2 tablespoons homemade Cashew Milk or store-bought dairy-free cashew milk**

**½ teaspoon sunflower lecithin**

**Pinch salt**

Place the coconut oil, cacao butter, oil, cashew milk, lecithin, and pinch salt in a high-speed blender and blend on high for 1 minute. Transfer to a resealable container and freeze until firm, about 30 minutes.

**Pumpkin Spice Pancakes with Cinnamon Maple Butter**

# CHAPTER THREE

# Smoothies & Breakfasts

Instant Yogurt

Smooth & Creamy Yogurt

Peanut Butter Split Smoothie

Coffee, Cinnamon & Spice Oats Smoothie

Berry-Mango Yogurt Smoothie

Tropical Coconut Yogurt Smoothie Bowl

15-Minute Buttermilk Pancakes

Pumpkin Spice Pancakes with Cinnamon Maple Butter

Honey-Oat Griddle Cakes

Peaches & Cream Cheese Pancakes

Strawberry Belgian Waffles with Easy Strawberry Syrup

Double Corn Muffins with Chive Butter

French Toast Bread Pudding with Maple Caramel

Caramel-Pecan Sticky Buns

# Snickerdoodle Apple Doughnut Muffins

# Instant Yogurt

5-INGREDIENT, EGG-FREE, FAMILY-FRIENDLY, GLUTEN-FREE, MAKE-AHEAD, VEGAN

MAKES 2 CUPS / PREP TIME: 3 MINUTES, PLUS 2 HOURS FOR RESTING AND REFRIGERATING

This recipe is as easy as turning on the blender and was inspired by the first dairy-free yogurt I ever tasted, at a juice bar in New York City. When I asked the manager what it was made of, I was surprised to learn it was young coconut meat, which comes from a green coconut—the soft, fleshy part of a mature brown coconut. The probiotics give the yogurt its characteristic tang. This yogurt keeps refrigerated in a resealable container for up to 1 week.

**2 cups young coconut meat**

**1 tablespoon plus 1 teaspoon date syrup**

**Seeds of 1 vanilla bean or 2 teaspoons pure vanilla extract**

**1 teaspoon dairy-free probiotic powder**

**¼ teaspoon salt**

**½ cup water**

Add the coconut meat, date syrup, vanilla seeds, probiotic powder, salt, and water to a high-speed blender; process on high speed until smooth. Let sit at room temperature until tangy, about 2 hours, then refrigerate until cold.

Time-saving Tip: For instant gratification, you can eat the yogurt right after blending. However, the longer the yogurt sits, the more tang you'll get.

# Smooth & Creamy Yogurt

**5-INGREDIENT, EGG-FREE, FAMILY-FRIENDLY, GLUTEN-FREE, MAKE-AHEAD, VEGAN**

**MAKES 1 QUART / PREP TIME: 8 MINUTES / COOK TIME: 20 MINUTES, PLUS 12 HOURS TO SET AND CHILL**

Dairy-free milks tend to have less natural sugar than cow's milk, so I've added sugar in this recipe, which helps with fermentation by providing food for the bacteria to grow. I culture the yogurt using a dairy-free starter culture—a live, active bacteria—that gives the yogurt its quintessential sourness. You do not need to buy a special candy thermometer or specialized type of thermometer for this recipe. I often use a simple meat thermometer to measure this mixture.

**4 cups homemade Cashew Milk or store-bought dairy-free cashew milk**

**2 tablespoons sugar**

**2¼ teaspoons (10 grams) iota carrageenan**

**¼ teaspoon dairy-free powdered yogurt starter culture**

1. In a medium saucepan, heat the milk and sugar over medium heat, whisking occasionally until the sugar is dissolved and a cooking thermometer reaches 110°.

2. Add the iota carrageenan, and, using an immersion blender, carefully blend to combine, about 1 minute.

3. Cook, whisking occasionally, until dissolved and the temperature reaches 140° and remove from the heat.

4. Let cool at room temperature, in the fridge, or set over an ice bath until the temperature reaches between 105° and 110°.

5. Add the dairy-free powdered yogurt starter culture and use an immersion blender to combine, about 30 seconds.

6. Strain the milk.

7. Using an electric yogurt maker, fill the glass jars about 1 inch from the rim, cap the jars, and place in the yogurt maker. Allow the milk to sit in the yogurt maker, undisturbed, until set and tangy, about 5 to 6 hours.

8. Let cool for at least 2 hours to return to room temperature, then refrigerate until completely chilled, about 6 hours or overnight.

9. To serve, use a fork to beat until smooth; refrigerate for up to 2 weeks.

# Peanut Butter Split Smoothie

**EGG-FREE, FAMILY-FRIENDLY, VEGAN**
**MAKES 1 SERVING / PREP TIME: 5 MINUTES**

There's no denying the one thing that will satisfy me—this thick and creamy smoothie. It's packed with protein and perfect for breakfast or a midafternoon pick-me-up. That said, it's so good, you could even call it dessert. I like to use coconut milk ice cubes that I make ahead of time with store-bought unsweetened coconut milk in ice cube trays for extra flavor and richness, but you can use regular ice cubes, too.

**1 cup coconut milk ice cubes or regular ice cubes**

**1 cup homemade <u>Cashew Milk</u> or <u>Oat Milk</u> or store-bought dairy-free cashew milk or oat milk**

**¼ cup peanut butter**

**1 ripe banana, preferably frozen, cut into 1-inch pieces**

**2 tablespoons cacao nibs (optional)**

**2 tablespoons coconut oil (optional)**

In a high-speed blender, blend together the ice cubes, milk, peanut butter, banana, cacao nibs (if using), and coconut oil (if using), until smooth.

Substitution Tip: **Not into peanut butter? Use almond butter instead. For a sweeter kick, try adding 1 teaspoon date syrup, maple syrup, or your other favorite sweetener.**

# Coffee, Cinnamon & Spice Oats Smoothie

EGG-FREE, FAMILY-FRIENDLY, VEGAN
MAKES 1 SERVING / PREP TIME: 5 MINUTES

This healthy spin on a smoothie will keep you full longer thanks to the fiber from the oats. When it comes to what liquid to add, it's up to you. Nut and oat milks add body and protein, but if you prefer something sweeter, try juice. If you want a lighter smoothie, go with coconut water. This coffee-buzzed breakfast smoothie will be extra smooth if you soak the nuts and oats in water overnight and then rinse and drain before using.

**1 ripe banana, preferably frozen, cut into 1-inch pieces**

**1 Medjool date, pitted**

**½ cup cold coffee**

**¼ cup raw cashews, soaked overnight, rinsed and drained**

**3 tablespoons old-fashioned rolled oats, soaked overnight, rinsed and drained**

**1 tablespoon unsweetened cocoa powder**

**¼ teaspoon cinnamon, to taste**

**Pinch cardamom**

**Pinch salt**

**½ cup ice cubes**

In a high-speed blender, blend together the banana, date, coffee, cashews, oats, cocoa powder, cinnamon, cardamom, salt, and ice until smooth.

Ingredient Tip: **For a stronger coffee flavor, try using cold-brew coffee.**

# Berry-Mango Yogurt Smoothie

EGG-FREE, FAMILY-FRIENDLY, GLUTEN-FREE, VEGAN
MAKES 1 SERVING / PREP TIME: 5 MINUTES

Tired of the same old yogurt for breakfast? This smoothie recipe gets a nice zing from freshly grated ginger. Want a thicker, more lassi-like consistency? Just reduce the liquid. This is a great base recipe for any fruit you love, so feel free to experiment with other frozen fruits. I use frozen fruit, so I don't need to add ice cubes, and the flavors won't get watered down.

**1 ripe banana, preferably frozen, cut into 1-inch pieces**

**1 cup frozen mixed berries**

**½ cup frozen mango chunks**

**¾ cup homemade Smooth & Creamy Yogurt or store-bought dairy-free plain yogurt**

**½ cup coconut water**

**1 teaspoon finely grated peeled ginger**

**1 Medjool date, pitted**

In a high-speed blender, blend together the banana, berries, mango, yogurt, coconut water, ginger, and date until smooth.

Cooking Tip: Save time in the mornings! This smoothie is perfect for prepping ahead of time. Just fill resealable freezer bags or containers with all of the smoothie ingredients, and you're ready to toss the entire contents in a blender and go.

# Tropical Coconut Yogurt Smoothie Bowl

**EGG-FREE, FAMILY-FRIENDLY, GLUTEN-FREE, VEGAN**
**MAKES 1 SERVING / PREP TIME: 5 MINUTES**

This recipe makes a refreshing, antioxidant-packed breakfast. Sometimes I add some granola at the end of blending for a bit of crunch. It may not seem intuitive to add salt to a breakfast item, but a pinch of salt makes everything taste better, including smoothie bowls.

½ **cup frozen pineapple chunks**

¼ **cup frozen mango chunks**

**1 (3.5-ounce) frozen unsweetened açai purée pack**

**1 cup homemade or store-bought dairy-free plain Instant Yogurt**

**1½ teaspoons finely grated peeled turmeric (optional)**

**Pinch salt**

**Pineapple chunks, mango slices, and unsweetened shredded coconut, for topping**

In a high-speed blender, purée together the pineapple, mango, açai, yogurt, tumeric (if using), and salt until smooth. Top with the pineapple, mango, and coconut.

Ingredient Tip: If you are looking for more protein, add 1 to 2 tablespoons of any nut butter or 1 scoop of dairy-free protein powder.

# 15-Minute Buttermilk Pancakes

FAMILY-FRIENDLY, NUT-FREE, VEGETARIAN
SERVES 4 / PREP TIME: 5 MINUTES / COOK TIME: 10 MINUTES

These classic pancakes are light and fluffy thanks to the buttermilk. Top the pancakes with your favorite berries, dairy-free chocolate chips, or even cooked bacon bits. Cooked pancakes will keep in resealable bags for up to 2 days in the refrigerator and 1 month in the freezer. For best results from frozen, defrost in the refrigerator overnight and reheat in a 350°F oven for 5 minutes.

**¾ cup plus 3 tablespoons all-purpose flour**

**1 tablespoon sugar**

**1½ teaspoons baking powder**

**¼ teaspoon baking soda**

**¼ teaspoon salt**

**1 large egg, at room temperature, or egg substitute**

**2 tablespoons neutral-flavored oil, plus more for greasing pan**

**¾ cup homemade Buttermilk or store-bought dairy-free buttermilk**

**1 teaspoon pure vanilla extract**

**Pure maple syrup, for serving**

1. In a small bowl, whisk together the flour, sugar, baking powder, baking soda, and salt.

2. In a separate medium bowl, add the flour mixture to the egg, oil, buttermilk, and vanilla and whisk together until smooth.

3. Heat a large nonstick skillet over medium-high heat and lightly grease with oil.

4. Pour the batter about ⅓ cup at a time onto the skillet and cook until golden and set, about 2 minutes on each side. Serve with maple syrup or your favorite toppings.

---

Substitution Tip: **Swap in any one of these vegan egg alternatives for the egg in this and other recipes. You may have to increase the cooking time by 5 minutes (see here).**

**AQUAFABA:** To make 1 large egg, use 3 tablespoons liquid from a can of unsalted chickpeas.

**CHIA EGG:** To make 1 large egg, stir together 1 tablespoon chia seed meal and 3 tablespoons hot water. Let sit until thickened, about 5 minutes.

**PSYLLIUM HUSK EGG:** To make 1 large egg, stir together 1 tablespoon psyllium husk powder and ¼ cup hot water. Let sit until thickened, about 5 minutes.

**GOLDEN FLAX EGG:** To make 1 large egg, stir together 1 tablespoon golden flaxseed meal and 3 tablespoons hot water. Let sit until thickened, about 10 minutes.

**STORE-BOUGHT VEGETARIAN EGG REPLACER POWDER:** Use according to package directions.

# Pumpkin Spice Pancakes with Cinnamon Maple Butter

FAMILY-FRIENDLY, MAKE-AHEAD, VEGETARIAN
SERVES 4 / PREP TIME: 10 MINUTES / COOK TIME: 16 MINUTES

These fluffy pancakes are full of spicy, warming fall flavors. You can also use canned pumpkin purée as a substitute for butter and oil in baking recipes. For this recipe, save time in the morning by preparing the cinnamon maple butter ahead of time so it's ready whenever you make your next batch of pancakes.

**FOR THE CINNAMON MAPLE BUTTER**

½ cup homemade Butter or store-bought dairy-free butter, at room temperature

2 tablespoons pure maple syrup

¼ teaspoon ground cinnamon

⅛ teaspoon salt

**FOR THE PANCAKES**

1½ cups all-purpose flour

2 tablespoons sugar

1 tablespoon baking powder

½ teaspoon salt

½ teaspoon pumpkin pie spice

1 cup homemade Cashew Milk or store-bought dairy-free cashew milk

½ cup canned pumpkin purée

¼ cup neutral-flavored oil, plus more for greasing pan

**2 large eggs or egg substitute (see tip), at room temperature**

**2 teaspoons pure vanilla extract**

### TO MAKE THE CINNAMON MAPLE BUTTER

In a small bowl, use a fork to combine the butter, maple syrup, cinnamon, and salt until smooth; refrigerate.

### TO MAKE THE PANCAKES

1. In a large bowl, whisk together the flour, sugar, baking powder, salt, and pumpkin pie spice.
2. In a separate medium bowl, whisk together the milk, pumpkin purée, oil, eggs, and vanilla.
3. Add the wet ingredients to the flour mixture and stir to combine.
4. Heat a large nonstick skillet over medium heat and lightly grease with oil.
5. Pour the batter about ¼ cup at a time onto the skillet and cook until golden and set, about 2 minutes on each side. Serve with the cinnamon maple butter.

Substitution Tip: Swap in sweet potato purée for the pumpkin for delicious sweet potato pancakes. An interesting fact about sweet potatoes is that they can help reduce inflammation due to their high quantities of beta-carotene, vitamin C, and magnesium.

# Honey-Oat Griddle Cakes

FAMILY-FRIENDLY, MAKE-AHEAD, VEGETARIAN
SERVES 4 / PREP TIME: 10 MINUTES / COOK TIME: 16 MINUTES

A take on one of my favorite childhood cereals, these griddle cakes are full of fiber and protein thanks to the oats and almond flour, which give the pancakes a tender crumb while keeping them airy and moist.

**1 cup all-purpose flour**

**¼ cup oat flour**

**¼ cup old-fashioned rolled oats**

**¼ cup almond flour**

**1 tablespoon baking powder**

**½ teaspoon salt**

**1¾ cups homemade Oat Milk or store-bought dairy-free unsweetened oat milk**

**2 large eggs or egg substitute (see tip), at room temperature**

**2 tablespoons neutral-flavored oil, plus more for greasing**

**2 tablespoons honey**

**2 teaspoons pure vanilla extract**

**½ teaspoon pure almond extract (optional)**

**Warm maple syrup, for serving**

1. In a large bowl, whisk together the all-purpose flour, oat flour, oats, almond flour, baking powder, and salt.

2. In a medium bowl, whisk together the milk, eggs, oil, honey, vanilla, and almond extract (if using); stir into the flour mixture

until just combined.

3. Heat a large nonstick skillet over medium heat and lightly grease with oil.

4. Pour the batter about ¼ cup at a time onto the skillet and spread to make 3-inch rounds. Cook until golden and set, about 2 minutes on each side. Serve with maple syrup.

# Peaches & Cream Cheese Pancakes

FAMILY-FRIENDLY, MAKE-AHEAD, VEGETARIAN
SERVES 4 / PREP TIME: 15 MINUTES / COOK TIME: 15 MINUTES

This flavor combination of fruit and cream cheese always reminds me of cheesecake. Who doesn't want dessert for breakfast sometimes? This dairy-free sweet pancake recipe is a staple in my house.

**1 cup all-purpose flour**

**½ cup blanched almond flour**

**2 tablespoons sugar**

**2 teaspoons baking powder**

**½ teaspoon salt**

**¾ cup homemade Cashew Milk or store-bought dairy-free cashew milk**

**2 large eggs or egg substitute (see tip), at room temperature**

**½ cup homemade Cream Cheese or store-bought dairy-free cream cheese, at room temperature**

**2 tablespoons neutral-flavored oil, plus more for greasing**

**2 teaspoons pure vanilla extract**

**1 cup finely chopped ripe peaches**

**Pure maple syrup, for serving**

1. In a blender, pulse together the all-purpose flour, almond flour, sugar, baking powder, and salt. Add the milk, eggs, cream cheese, oil, and vanilla; blend until combined. Transfer to a bowl and stir in the peaches by hand.

2. Heat a large nonstick skillet over medium heat and lightly grease with oil.

3. Pour the batter about ¼ cup at a time onto the skillet and cook until golden and set, about 2 minutes on each side. Serve with maple syrup.

---

Substitution Tip: **Swap in strawberries for the peaches for the ultimate strawberry cheesecake in pancake form, or use any other berry or fruit you have in the fridge.**

# Strawberry Belgian Waffles with Easy Strawberry Syrup

FAMILY-FRIENDLY, MAKE-AHEAD, VEGETARIAN
SERVES 4 / PREP TIME: 5 MINUTES / COOK TIME: 8 MINUTES

The sweet smell of waffles baking always brings me back to the kitchen wanting more. All of those crispy crevices help, too. No waffle iron? Make pancakes instead. Just add more liquid to get your preferred pancake batter consistency. These waffles can be frozen in an airtight container for up to 1 month.

**1¾ cups plus 2 tablespoons all-purpose flour (used all at once)**

**2 tablespoons sugar**

**1 tablespoon baking powder**

**½ teaspoon salt**

**1⅓ cups homemade Cashew Milk or store-bought dairy-free cashew milk**

**2 large eggs or egg substitute (see tip), at room temperature**

**¼ cup neutral-flavored oil**

**1 tablespoon pure vanilla extract**

**¾ cup chopped strawberries**

**1 cup strawberry jelly**

**¼ cup water**

1. Preheat a Belgian waffle iron to medium-high heat.
2. In a small bowl, whisk together the flour, sugar, baking powder, and salt.
3. In a large bowl, whisk together the milk, eggs, oil, and vanilla.

Add the flour mixture and whisk until just combined. Gently stir in the strawberries.

4. Grease the waffle iron with dairy-free nonstick cooking spray.

5. Pour a heaping ⅓ cup batter into each waffle iron quarter, spreading the batter out to the edges. Close and cook until crisp, about 4 minutes. Repeat with the remaining batter.

6. While the waffles are cooking, in a small saucepan, cook the jelly and water over low heat, stirring occasionally until syrupy. Serve with the waffles.

Substitution Tip: If you have pancake mix in your pantry, go ahead and swap in 2 cups of pancake mix for the homemade version in the recipe.

# Double Corn Muffins with Chive Butter

FAMILY-FRIENDLY, MAKE-AHEAD, VEGETARIAN
MAKES 12 / PREP TIME: 5 MINUTES / COOK TIME: 20 MINUTES

There's something about combining cornmeal and fresh corn kernels that makes these muffins buttery—even though there's no traditional dairy butter in the recipe. When I serve these corn muffins warm with chive butter to my family and friends, there are never any leftovers. These double corn muffins are sure to be a hit.

### FOR THE DOUBLE CORN MUFFINS

1 cup cornmeal, preferably medium grind

1 cup all-purpose flour

¼ cup sugar

1 tablespoon baking powder

1 teaspoon baking soda

1 teaspoon salt

1 cup homemade Buttermilk or store-bought dairy-free buttermilk

2 large eggs or egg substitute (see tip), at room temperature

¼ cup neutral-flavored oil

1 cup fresh or thawed frozen corn kernels

### FOR THE CHIVE BUTTER

½ cup homemade Butter or store-bought dairy-free butter, at room temperature

¼ cup finely chopped chives

**Pinch salt**

### TO MAKE THE DOUBLE CORN MUFFINS

1. Preheat the oven to 350°F and line a 12-cup muffin pan with paper liners.

2. In a medium bowl, whisk together the cornmeal, flour, sugar, baking powder, baking soda, and salt.

3. Stir in the buttermilk, eggs, and oil until just blended; fold in the corn kernels.

4. Pour the batter into the prepared muffin pan; bake until golden and a toothpick inserted in the center of a muffin comes out clean, about 20 minutes. Let cool completely in the pan set on a wire rack.

### TO MAKE THE CHIVE BUTTER

1. Using a food processor or a fork, blend together the butter, chives, and salt until smooth.

2. Line a small bowl with plastic wrap and fill with the butter mixture; cover with the plastic and refrigerate until ready to serve.

# French Toast Bread Pudding with Maple Caramel

FAMILY-FRIENDLY, MAKE-AHEAD, VEGETARIAN
SERVES 6 / PREP TIME: 10 MINUTES / COOK TIME: 20 MINUTES

This is my quick, fun spin on classic French toast with maple syrup baked in. In this recipe, you'll use a water bath when baking, which adds moisture to the oven and helps food bake at an even temperature. I like using store-bought cinnamon swirl bread, but you can also use your favorite bread, such as plain white or cinnamon-raisin.

**1 cup sugar**

**2 tablespoons plus ¼ cup pure maple syrup (2 tablespoons used first, then ¼ cup used later)**

**½ cup water**

**2 cups homemade Cashew Milk or store-bought dairy-free cashew milk**

**2 large eggs or egg substitute (see tip), at room temperature**

**7 slices stale store-bought dairy-free cinnamon swirl bread, toasted and torn into pieces**

1. Preheat the oven to 400°F. Butter a 9-by-2-inch round cake pan.

2. In a small, heavy saucepan, bring the sugar, 2 tablespoons of maple syrup, and water to a boil over medium-high heat, without stirring, and cook for 5 minutes. Boil until the caramel is a light golden color, about 5 minutes more; pour into the prepared cake pan.

3. In a large bowl, whisk together the milk, eggs, and remaining ¼

cup maple syrup. Soak the bread pieces in the custard until moistened, then place the bread on top of the maple caramel in the cake pan, pressing down gently to flatten. Pour any remaining custard over the bread.

4. Set the cake pan in a large roasting pan and carefully pour enough hot water into the roasting pan to reach halfway up the sides of the cake pan. Bake until the bread is golden, the custard is set, and a toothpick inserted in the center comes out clean, about 20 minutes. Remove the bread pudding from the water bath, cut into wedges, and serve warm.

Cooking Tip: To make individual portions of this delicious breakfast favorite, add ingredients to separate individual ramekins or small bowls in the same order and check with a toothpick after 10 minutes of baking time.

# Caramel-Pecan Sticky Buns

5-INGREDIENT, FAMILY-FRIENDLY, MAKE-AHEAD, VEGETARIAN
MAKES 12 / PREP TIME: 10 MINUTES / BAKE TIME: 20 MINUTES

This recipe gives you freshly baked sticky buns in just 30 minutes. To prepare these ahead of time, you can assemble the entire recipe the night before, then just let the dough come to room temperature before baking.

**12 tablespoons homemade Butter or store-bought dairy-free butter, at room temperature, plus 2 tablespoons melted and cooled (12 tablespoons used first, then 1 tablespoon used later for each pastry)**

**¾ cup brown sugar (¼ cup used first, then ¼ cup used later for each pastry)**

**1½ cups pecans, chopped**

**1 package (2 sheets) frozen puff pastry, defrosted**

**2 teaspoons cinnamon**

1. Preheat the oven to 400°F and place a 12-cup muffin pan on a baking sheet.
2. Using a handheld mixer, combine 12 tablespoons butter and ¼ cup brown sugar.
3. Place a tablespoon of the mixture in the bottom of each muffin cup and sprinkle with about one-third of the chopped pecans.
4. Lightly flour a clean, dry surface and, working one at a time, unfold 1 sheet of puff pastry with the folds going left to right. Brush with 1 tablespoon melted butter, leaving a 1-inch border.
5. Sprinkle with ¼ cup brown sugar, 1 teaspoon cinnamon, and ½ cup pecans.

6. Starting with the end nearest you, roll up the puff pastry, jelly-roll style, finishing seam-side down; trim the ends and cut into six 1½-inch pieces.

7. Place each piece, cut-side down, in 6 of the muffin cups. Repeat steps 4 through 6 with the remaining dough and filling.

8. Bake until golden, about 20 minutes. Let cool for 3 minutes, then immediately invert onto parchment paper and let cool completely.

# Snickerdoodle Apple Doughnut Muffins

FAMILY-FRIENDLY, VEGETARIAN

MAKES 12 / PREP TIME: 10 MINUTES / COOK TIME: 20 MINUTES

These baked muffins taste like fresh-out-of-the-fryer, old-fashioned doughnuts rolled in sweet cinnamon sugar. I love the chopped apples in this batter for a perfect fall breakfast treat.

**FOR THE CRUMB MIXTURE**

¼ cup brown sugar

2 teaspoons all-purpose flour

⅛ teaspoon salt

½ teaspoon cinnamon

**FOR THE MUFFINS**

1½ cups all-purpose flour

½ cup granulated sugar

¼ cup brown sugar

2 teaspoons baking powder

½ teaspoon salt

½ teaspoon cinnamon

2 large eggs or egg substitute (see tip), at room temperature

6 tablespoons cooled melted homemade Butter or store-bought dairy-free butter

¼ cup homemade Cashew Milk or store-bought dairy-free cashew milk

1 teaspoon pure vanilla extract

1 large apple, cored, peeled, and cut into ¼-inch pieces

**FOR THE TOPPING**

½ cup granulated sugar

2 teaspoons cinnamon

6 tablespoons cooled melted homemade <u>Butter</u> or store-bought dairy-free butter

**TO MAKE THE CRUMB MIXTURE**

In a small bowl, stir together the brown sugar, flour, salt, and cinnamon.

**TO MAKE THE MUFFINS**

1. Preheat the oven to 350°F and line a 12-cup muffin pan with paper liners.
2. In a large bowl, whisk together the flour, granulated sugar, brown sugar, baking powder, salt, and cinnamon.
3. In a medium bowl, whisk together the eggs, melted butter, milk, and vanilla until smooth; add to the flour mixture and stir to combine.
4. Fold in the apple and the crumb mixture.
5. Divide the batter among the prepared muffin cups until about three-quarters full; bake until a toothpick inserted comes out clean, about 20 minutes.

**TO MAKE THE TOPPING**

1. In a small bowl, stir together the granulated sugar and cinnamon.

2. Place the melted butter in another small bowl.

3. While still warm out of the oven, dip each muffin top into the butter first, then coat with cinnamon sugar.

---

Substitution Tip: If apples aren't your favorite, try this muffin with other flavors, like pineapple for a summer vibe or cranberries for a cozy winter taste. Make sure to check the doneness of your muffins after 12 minutes when using different fruits, as the moisture levels are different and may make your muffins cook a little faster or slower.

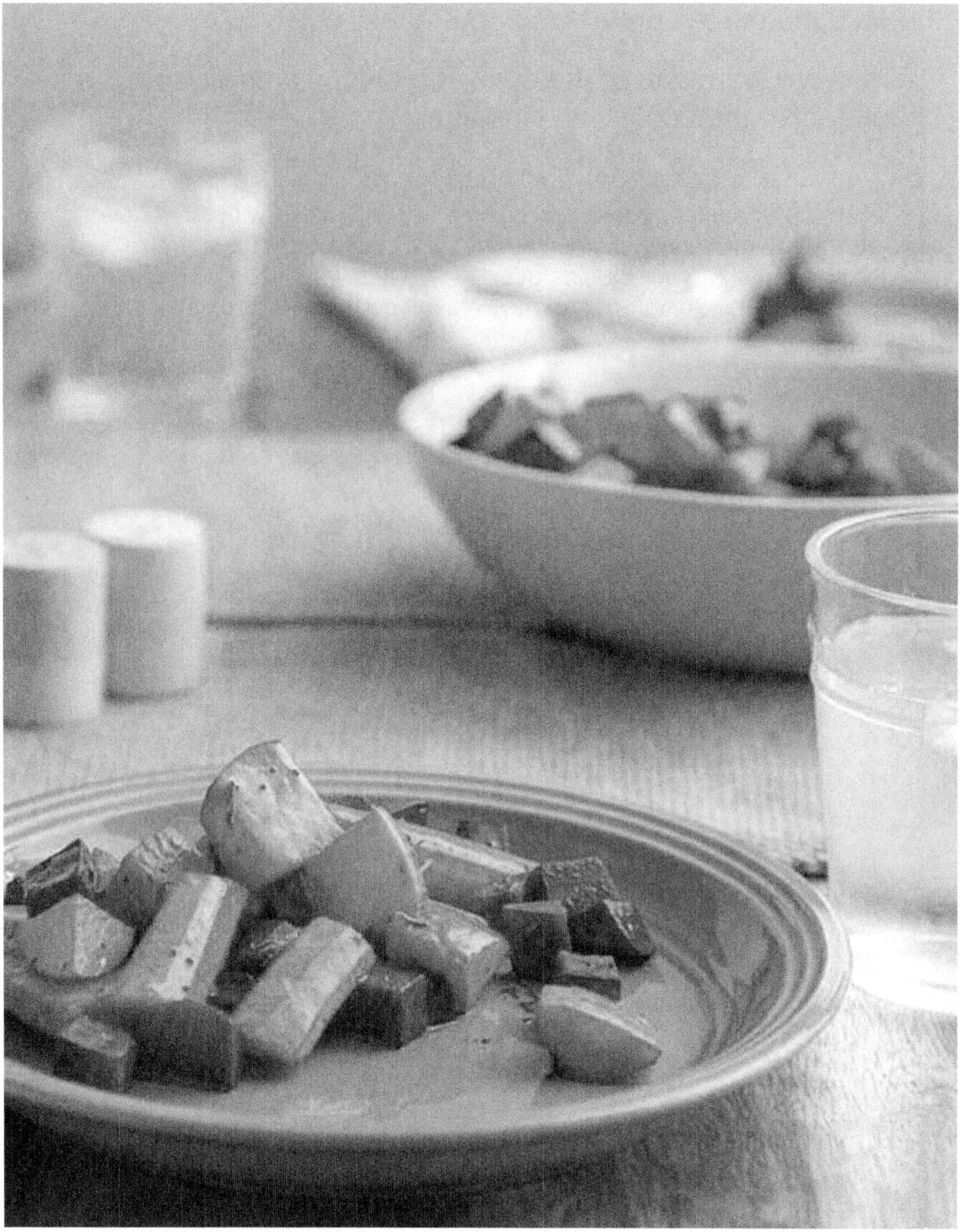

## Warm Roasted Beet, Carrot & Apple Salad with Creamy Poppy Seed Vinaigrette

# CHAPTER FOUR

# Soups & Salads

Tomato Alphabet Bisque

Gingery Carrot & Cashew Bisque

Creamy Corn Soup with Crispy Bacon

Cream of Mushroom Soup

Basmati Chicken-Ginger Meatball Soup

Avocado Gazpacho

Creamy Ranch Summer Pasta Salad

Philly Steak Salad Bowls

Vietnamese-Style Pork Lettuce Wraps

Shrimp Scampi Caesar Salad

Warm Roasted Beet, Carrot & Apple Salad with Creamy Poppy Seed Vinaigrette

Wedge Salad with Avocado Ranch Dressing & Chickpea Croutons

# Tomato Alphabet Bisque

EGG-FREE, FAMILY-FRIENDLY, MAKE-AHEAD, ONE-POT, VEGETARIAN
SERVES 4 TO 6 / PREP TIME: 5 MINUTES / COOK TIME: 25 MINUTES

The bisque is thickened with cooked quinoa in place of dairy and then blended until creamy. The honey cuts the tomatoes' acidity and adds just a touch of sweetness. Alphabet pasta is a fun touch that kids love, but any type of small pasta shapes will work in this recipe.

1 tablespoon olive oil

½ medium onion, chopped

2 garlic cloves, chopped

2 carrots, chopped into small pieces

1 (28-ounce) can diced tomatoes with juice

4 cups vegetable broth or water

½ cup cooked quinoa

½ cup homemade Cashew Milk or store-bought dairy-free cashew milk

1½ teaspoons honey

1 cup uncooked alphabet pasta

**Salt**

**Freshly ground black pepper**

1. In a large pot, heat the oil over medium heat. Add the onion, garlic, and carrots; cook, stirring occasionally, until softened, about 8 minutes.

2. Reserve ¼ cup of the tomatoes and drain only those. Add the remaining tomatoes with their juice and the broth; cover and bring to a boil.

3. Stir in the quinoa and simmer for 10 minutes.

4. Using an immersion blender, purée until smooth.

5. Stir in the reserved tomatoes, milk, and honey. Return to a boil and stir in the pasta.

6. Reduce the heat to low and simmer until pasta is al dente, about 7 minutes. Season with salt and pepper.

---

Substitution Tip: Swap in cooked rice for the quinoa for a similar texture.

# Gingery Carrot & Cashew Bisque

EGG-FREE, FAMILY-FRIENDLY, GLUTEN-FREE, MAKE-AHEAD, ONE-POT, VEGAN
SERVES 4 TO 6 / PREP TIME: 5 MINUTES / COOK TIME: 24 MINUTES

Raw cashews are the secret to the creaminess that makes this soup a bisque. Lime is the other curious ingredient that lifts all the flavors and adds a tasty zing in an otherwise simple vegetable soup.

**2 tablespoons olive oil**

**1 onion, chopped**

**1 pound carrots, chopped into small pieces**

**1 cup raw cashews, soaked in boiling water for 15 minutes, rinsed and drained**

**1 (1-inch) piece fresh ginger, peeled and chopped**

**4 cups vegetable broth or water**

**½ cup homemade Cashew Milk or store-bought dairy-free cashew milk**

**½ cup fresh parsley**

**Juice of 2 limes**

**Salt**

1. Heat the oil in a large pot over medium heat. Add the onion and carrots; cook, stirring occasionally, until softened, about 8 minutes.
2. Add the cashews, ginger, and broth; bring to a boil. Simmer, covered, until the carrots are tender, about 15 minutes.
3. Stir in the milk and parsley.

4. Using an immersion blender, purée until smooth, about 1 minute. To serve, stir in the lime juice and season with salt.

---

Cooking Tip: If you have a high-speed blender, you can make this bisque in just over 5 minutes. Cook the onions and put them in the blender along with the carrots, cashews, ginger, broth, and cashew milk; blend in batches if necessary, until smooth and hot, about 1 minute. Add the parsley and blend until chopped, about 5 seconds. To serve, stir in the lime juice and season with salt.

# Creamy Corn Soup with Crispy Bacon

EGG-FREE, GLUTEN-FREE, MAKE-AHEAD, NUT-FREE, ONE-POT
SERVES 4 / PREP TIME: 10 MINUTES / COOK TIME: 20 MINUTES

Corn chowder may be a summer comfort food, especially in the Northeast when just-picked corn is everywhere, but the star ingredient here is the cannellini beans, which give this soup an undeniably creamy, classic consistency.

**2 slices bacon**

**2 tablespoons olive oil**

**1 small onion, finely chopped**

**2 celery stalks, cut into ¼-inch pieces**

**1 potato, peeled and cut into ½-inch pieces**

**4 ears corn, kernels removed, about 4 cups (3 cups used first, 1 cup used later)**

**1 (15-ounce) can cannellini beans, drained, rinsed, and mashed until creamy**

**3 cups vegetable broth or water**

**1 cup homemade Cashew Milk Creamer (see tip) or store-bought dairy-free creamer**

**Salt**

**Freshly ground black pepper**

**Fresh chives, chopped, for topping**

**Hot sauce for serving (optional)**

1. In a skillet, cook the bacon over medium heat until crispy and the fat has rendered, about 3 minutes. Using a slotted spoon,

remove from the pan and drain on paper towels. Crumble into small pieces.

2. In a large pot, heat the olive oil over medium-high heat. Add the onion and celery; cook until softened, about 3 minutes.

3. Add the potato, 3 cups of corn kernels, cannellini beans, broth, and creamer; bring to a boil. Reduce the heat to medium and simmer until the potato is tender, about 14 minutes; season with salt and pepper.

4. Using an immersion blender, partially purée until smooth but still chunky. Divide the soup among four bowls and top with the remaining 1 cup of corn, chives, and hot sauce (if using).

Cooking Tip: Save time by swapping in 4 cups thawed frozen corn kernels for the fresh ears of corn.

# Cream of Mushroom Soup

EGG-FREE, GLUTEN-FREE, MAKE-AHEAD, ONE-POT, VEGAN
SERVES 4 TO 6 / PREP TIME: 5 MINUTES / COOK TIME: 25 MINUTES

I grew up on Campbell's Condensed Cream of Mushroom Soup, but there's no turning back now that I've perfected my own easy and super flavorful version. I prefer my soup thick and creamy, but you can add ½ cup more broth or water if you prefer your soup a bit thinner.

**6½ cups (1¼ pounds) fresh button mushrooms, trimmed and sliced**

**½ onion, chopped**

**3 garlic cloves, unpeeled**

**4 fresh rosemary sprigs**

**3 tablespoons olive oil**

**Salt**

**Freshly ground black pepper**

**3 cups vegetable broth or water**

**1 cup homemade Cashew Milk Creamer (see tip) or store-bought dairy-free creamer**

**1 potato, peeled and cut into ½-inch pieces**

1. Preheat the oven to 400°F.
2. Place the mushrooms, onion, garlic, and rosemary on a baking sheet. Drizzle with olive oil and season with salt and pepper; toss to coat and spread out in a single layer. Roast, stirring occasionally, until tender, about 15 minutes; squeeze the garlic cloves from their skins.

3. Transfer the roasted vegetables to a large pot and add the broth, creamer, and potato; bring to a boil over medium-high heat.

4. Reduce the heat to medium and simmer until the potato is tender, about 10 minutes; remove and discard the rosemary.

5. Using an immersion blender, purée until smooth.

---

Ingredient Tip: **Button mushrooms are also called "white mushrooms" and are the most common mushrooms available at supermarkets. You can also use dried mushrooms and reconstitute them. When doing the conversion for 1¼ pound of fresh to dried mushrooms, use just over 3½ ounces of dried and reconstituted mushrooms.**

# Basmati Chicken-Ginger Meatball Soup

ONE-POT, EGG-FREE, GLUTEN-FREE, MAKE-AHEAD, NUT-FREE
SERVES 4 TO 6 / PREP TIME: 10 MINUTES / COOK TIME: 15 MINUTES

This soup takes chicken soup to the next level with the surprisingly satisfying chicken meatballs, which are packed with basmati rice, ginger, and garlic. It has the comfort and wholesomeness of traditional chicken soup but with more of a kick and new flavors. I love making a big pot of this and freezing it for an easy meal.

6 cups homemade or store-bought low-sodium chicken broth

1 pound ground chicken

2 teaspoons grated fresh ginger

1 garlic clove, finely chopped

¼ cup fresh spinach, finely chopped

½ teaspoon salt

¼ teaspoon pepper

1 large egg or egg substitute (see tip), beaten

⅓ cup uncooked basmati rice

1. In a large soup pot, bring the broth to a boil; reduce the heat to low and simmer.

2. In a medium bowl, combine the ground chicken, ginger, garlic, spinach, salt, pepper, egg, and rice; roll into 1-inch balls.

3. Carefully add the meatballs to the hot broth; cover and cook until the chicken and rice are cooked through, about 15 minutes.

Serve hot.

---

Substitution Tip: No basmati rice? No worries. Just swap in whatever rice you already have on hand for the same texture. Brown rice is a great substitute and is packed with fiber.

# Avocado Gazpacho

EGG-FREE, GLUTEN-FREE, MAKE-AHEAD, NUT-FREE, ONE-POT, VEGAN
SERVES: 4 TO 6 / PREP TIME: 15 MINUTES, PLUS 3 HOURS TO CHILL

I like to serve this cold summer soup with crushed tortilla chips. Make it dinner by topping the gazpacho with poached shrimp or lobster. If the gazpacho thickens too much, gradually add water until it reaches your desired consistency. This recipe is over 30 minutes because of needing to chill it, but the ingredients come together quickly for a refreshing and satisfying cold soup.

½ pound chopped watermelon

3 large tomatoes (about 2 pounds), cored and chopped

1 small onion, chopped

1 bell pepper, seeded and chopped

1 cucumber, peeled, seeded, and chopped

2 cups tomato juice

2 tablespoons lime juice

1 cup cooked corn kernels

2 avocados, peeled and chopped

Salt

Freshly ground black pepper

1 jalapeño, seeded and chopped

¼ cup fresh cilantro or parsley, chopped

Lime wedges, for serving

1. In a blender, purée the watermelon and then strain through a sieve set over a bowl. You should have about 1 cup of juice.

2. Working in batches, place the tomatoes, onion, pepper, and cucumber in the bowl of a food processor and pulse until chunky.

3. Transfer to a large bowl and stir in the tomato juice, watermelon juice, and lime juice. Stir in the corn and avocados; season with salt and pepper and refrigerate until completely chilled, at least 3 hours or overnight.

4. After it is chilled, stir in the jalapeño (to taste) and cilantro; serve with lime wedges.

Substitution Tip: Have orange juice in the fridge? Swap it in for the homemade watermelon juice. For a smooth garnish, top this gazpacho with a dollop of scallion sour cream. Just stir together 1 cup homemade Sour Cream or store-bought dairy-free sour cream with 4 finely chopped scallions and season with salt and pepper.

# Creamy Ranch Summer Pasta Salad

EGG-FREE, FAMILY-FRIENDLY, MAKE-AHEAD, VEGAN
SERVES 4 TO 6 / PREP TIME: 8 MINUTES / COOK TIME: 11 MINUTES

I've swapped in a quick creamy cashew ranch dressing for heavy mayo in this summer veggie-packed macaroni salad. This dish is great for a potluck or summer block party and no one will even know it is dairy-free!

**2½ cups (8 ounces) short pasta, such as fusilli or penne**

**Neutral-flavored oil, for drizzling**

**1 celery stalk, finely chopped**

**1 red bell pepper, seeded and chopped**

**1 medium carrot, grated**

**1 ear corn, kernels removed**

**2 tablespoons finely chopped red onion**

**1 tablespoon finely chopped parsley**

**1 recipe homemade Ranch Dressing or store-bought dairy-free ranch dressing**

1. In a large saucepan of boiling salted water, cook the pasta until al dente, about 12 minutes; drain and rinse with cold water.

2. Spread the cooked pasta evenly on a baking sheet, drizzle with oil, and toss; let cool completely.

3. In a large bowl, toss together the cooled pasta, celery, bell pepper, carrot, corn, onion, and parsley. Add the ranch dressing

and toss to combine.

---

Ingredient Tip: Want to add some greens? Stir some chopped kale or spinach into the salad along with the other veggies.

# Philly Steak Salad Bowls

EGG-FREE, GLUTEN-FREE, NUT-FREE
SERVES 4 / PREP TIME: 10 MINUTES / COOK TIME: 5 MINUTES

For extra flavor, I sometimes stir some garlic powder into the steak. I also like to serve this as a cold salad by refrigerating the steak until cold and topping with shredded cheese, no melting necessary.

**2 tablespoons olive oil, plus more for drizzling**

**1 red bell pepper, stemmed, ribs and seeds removed and sliced lengthwise**

**1 pound steak stir-fry strips**

**Salt**

**Freshly ground black pepper**

**1 cup shredded dairy-free mozzarella cheese**

**1 head iceberg lettuce, chopped**

**Vinegar**

1. In a skillet, heat the oil over medium-high heat and cook the bell pepper and steak until the peppers are tender, about 5 minutes; season with salt and pepper. Turn off the heat and scatter the cheese on top; let melt.

2. Remove the outer leaves of the lettuce and coarsely chop; divide between 4 bowls and drizzle lightly with oil and vinegar to taste and season with salt and pepper. Top each bowl with a quarter of the steak mixture.

Cooking Tip: If you enjoy lettuce wraps, try serving the steak and peppers on a large leaf of iceberg or Boston lettuce and wrap instead of as a salad.

# Vietnamese-Style Pork Lettuce Wraps

**EGG-FREE, MAKE-AHEAD**
MAKES 12 (2-INCH) PATTIES / PREP TIME: 10 MINUTES / COOK TIME: 8 MINUTES

Lettuce is a light and crunchy wrapper for summer, and these wraps are fresh and fun with great Vietnamese flavors. For some heat and an extra kick, I like to stir hot sauce into the patty mixture. You can serve these lettuce wraps hot or at room temperature.

**FOR THE PATTIES**

1 pound ground pork

2 scallions, thinly sliced crosswise

1 garlic clove, finely chopped

1 tablespoon soy sauce

1 teaspoon sesame oil

½ teaspoon salt

¼ teaspoon pepper

2 tablespoons olive oil

**FOR THE SAUCE**

2 teaspoons vinegar

1 teaspoon soy sauce

½ teaspoon sesame oil

2 cups coleslaw mix

Salt

**Freshly ground black pepper**

**12 Boston lettuce leaves**

**Chopped mint, cilantro, or basil, for topping**

### TO MAKE THE PATTIES

1. In a medium bowl, mix the pork, scallions, garlic, soy sauce, sesame oil, salt, and pepper; form into 12 (2-inch) patties.

2. In a large skillet, heat the olive oil over medium heat and cook the burgers, turning once, until cooked through, about 4 minutes on each side or until the patties feel firm or a thermometer reads 160°F.

### TO MAKE THE SAUCE

1. In a medium bowl, whisk together the vinegar, soy sauce, and sesame oil. Add the coleslaw mix, toss together; season with salt and pepper.

2. To serve, stack the lettuce leaves on plates and divide the pork patties and coleslaw onto the lettuce leaves. Top each wrap with chopped herbs.

Cooking Tip: You can grill the patties and use slider rolls in place of the lettuce for a more cookout-friendly recipe.

# Shrimp Scampi Caesar Salad

EGG-FREE, FAMILY-FRIENDLY, MAKE-AHEAD, VEGAN
SERVES 4 / PREP TIME: 10 MINUTES / COOK TIME: 8 MINUTES

The modified Caesar salad dressing in this recipe contains no egg but tastes just as good—if not better—than the original. Make the dressing ahead of time and store in an airtight container in the refrigerator for up to 1 week.

**1 pound shrimp, shelled**

**2 tablespoons olive oil**

**2 tablespoons dry vermouth or white wine (optional)**

**1 tablespoon lemon juice**

**2 garlic cloves, finely chopped**

**2 tablespoons finely chopped fresh parsley**

**½ teaspoon salt**

**¼ teaspoon pepper**

**1 head romaine lettuce, quartered lengthwise and cut crosswise into ½-inch strips**

**¾ cup homemade Caesar Parmesan Dressing or store-bought dairy-free Caesar dressing**

**1 teaspoon lemon zest**

**Homemade or store-bought croutons, for serving (optional)**

1. In a medium bowl, toss together the shrimp, oil, vermouth (if using), lemon juice, garlic, parsley, salt, and pepper; refrigerate for 10 minutes.

2. Heat the broiler to high. Place the shrimp on a foil-lined baking

sheet; broil, turning once, until the shrimp is opaque, about 4 minutes total.

3. Place the lettuce in a large bowl and toss with the dressing. Divide evenly into 4 bowls and top with the shrimp, lemon zest, and croutons (if using).

---

Ingredient Tip: If you have stale bread, you can make your own croutons. Just preheat the oven to 325°F and toss bread chopped into cubes with oil and spread on a baking sheet; bake until crisp and golden, about 15 minutes. Let cool on a paper towel–lined plate. Store in an airtight container for up to 1 week.

# Warm Roasted Beet, Carrot & Apple Salad with Creamy Poppy Seed Vinaigrette

EGG-FREE, GLUTEN-FREE, MAKE-AHEAD, VEGAN
SERVES 4 / PREP TIME: 10 MINUTES / COOK TIME: 15 MINUTES

This salad feels and smells like fall with the warm root vegetables and apples. The macadamia nut–based poppy seed vinaigrette lifts all the flavors. Add a hint of heat and depth with a pinch of cayenne.

**3 medium beets (about 1 pound), peeled and cut into ½-inch pieces**

**¼ cup olive oil, plus more for drizzling**

**6 large carrots (about 1 pound), peeled and cut lengthwise then into 1-inch pieces**

**1 large red apple, cut into large chunks**

**4 thyme sprigs**

**Salt**

**Freshly ground black pepper**

**¾ cup homemade Creamy Poppy Seed Vinaigrette or store-bought dairy-free creamy poppy seed vinaigrette**

1. Preheat the oven to 400°F. Place the beets on a baking sheet, drizzle with olive oil, toss, and cover with foil. Bake until tender, about 15 minutes.

2. On a separate baking sheet, place the carrots, apple, and thyme; drizzle with olive oil, season with salt and pepper, and toss; cover with foil. Bake until tender, about 15 minutes.

3. Add the beets, carrots, and apple to a large bowl. Drizzle over the dressing and toss to coat; season with salt and pepper if needed.

---

Ingredient Tip: If you want to add meat to this salad, ground pork goes well with these flavors. Try using 1 pound of ground pork cooked over medium-high heat until browned. Drain the juices and add to the salad. For another nonmeat option, add cooked lentils to this salad.

# Wedge Salad with Avocado Ranch Dressing & Chickpea Croutons

EGG-FREE, GLUTEN-FREE, MAKE-AHEAD, VEGAN
SERVES 4 / PREP TIME: 8 MINUTES / COOK TIME: 15 MINUTES

Avocado transforms everyday ranch dressing into a cooling summer dressing. If you're making the dressing ahead of time, cover it with plastic wrap so that it sits directly on the surface and refrigerate to avoid browning.

1 (15.5-ounce) can chickpeas, rinsed and drained

2 tablespoons olive oil

¼ teaspoon cayenne pepper

½ teaspoon salt

¼ teaspoon pepper

1½ cups homemade Ranch Dressing or store-bought dairy-free ranch dressing

1 avocado, halved, pitted, and peeled

2 scallions, chopped

½ garlic clove

2 teaspoons lemon juice

1 head iceberg lettuce, cut into 8 wedges

2 tablespoons chives, for topping

1. Preheat the oven to 400°F.

2. On a rimmed baking sheet, toss the chickpeas with the oil, cayenne pepper, salt, and pepper. Bake, shaking the pan occasionally, until golden and crisp, about 15 minutes.

3. Meanwhile, in a blender or food processor, blend together the ranch dressing, avocado, scallions, garlic, and lemon juice until smooth; season with salt and pepper.

4. To serve, place the lettuce wedges on a platter, drizzle with the dressing, and top with the chickpea croutons and chives.

Substitution Tip: The chickpea croutons add a wonderful crunch, but go ahead and use regular croutons if you prefer.

**Cream Cheese & Cheddar Stuffed Jalapeño Poppers**

# CHAPTER FIVE

# Snacks & Sides

Potato Chips with Caramelized Onion Dip

Veggie Crudité with Avocado-Hummus Dip

Cream Cheese & Cheddar Stuffed Jalapeño Poppers

Tortilla Chips with Chipotle Cheese Fondue

Double-Baked Sour Cream & Chive Potatoes

Three-Cheese Garlic Bread

Bacon–Brussels Sprouts Hash

Cinnamon-Raisin Bread Breakfast Sausage Stuffing

Chinese-Style Honey-Mustard Chicken Wings

Ranch Chicken Nuggets

# Potato Chips with Caramelized Onion Dip

EGG-FREE, MAKE-AHEAD
SERVES 4 / PREP TIME: 5 MINUTES / COOK TIME: 20 MINUTES

I love serving this easy dip for any party occasion, especially because I can make it ahead of time and have it ready to serve when guests arrive. Caramelizing onions makes this onion dip full of flavor. I prefer using red onion, but you could use any onion you have on hand. The onion dip can be covered and refrigerated for up to 3 days.

**2 tablespoons olive oil**

**2 large red onions, cut into thin rounds, then quartered**

**1 garlic clove, finely chopped**

**½ teaspoon Worcestershire sauce**

**¼ teaspoon salt**

**⅛ teaspoon pepper**

**½ cup homemade Sour Cream or store-bought dairy-free sour cream**

**1 teaspoon soy sauce**

**1 tablespoon water**

**Potato chips, for serving**

1. Heat a large skillet over medium-high heat. Add the olive oil, onions, garlic, Worcestershire sauce, salt, and pepper and cook, stirring occasionally, until the onions are softened, about 10 minutes. Reduce the heat to medium-low and cook until golden, about 10 minutes more.

2. Using a blender, purée together ¼ cup of the caramelized onions, sour cream, and soy sauce; add 1 tablespoon water for a dip consistency (if necessary). Transfer to a bowl.

3. Stir in the remaining caramelized onions and season with salt and pepper; serve immediately with potato chips or refrigerate until ready to eat.

---

Ingredient Tip: If you have time, go ahead and make your own potato chips. Preheat the oven to 400°F. Using a mandoline, slice 2 peeled Yukon Gold potatoes into ⅛-inch slices and place on a baking sheet. Toss with 3 tablespoons olive oil and season with salt; arrange the slices in a single layer and bake until golden brown, about 12 minutes. Season again with salt and transfer to a rack to cool.

# Veggie Crudité with Avocado-Hummus Dip

CALCIUM-RICH, EGG-FREE, GLUTEN-FREE, MAKE-AHEAD, NUT-FREE, VEGAN
SERVES 4 / PREP TIME: 10 MINUTES

Avocado may seem destined for guacamole stardom, but this fruit also gives any recipe a creamy texture and a pillowy lightness, which creates a fun spin on traditional hummus. I listed the veggies I prefer for this dip, but you can use any veggies you prefer. Try topping the dip with pitted chopped kalamata olives and a pinch of dried oregano for a Greek flair. The dip can be made up to 4 days ahead. Transfer to an airtight container, cover the surface with plastic, and refrigerate.

4 garlic cloves, unpeeled

2 ripe avocados, halved, pitted, and peeled

1 (15-ounce) can chickpeas, drained and rinsed

¼ cup olive oil, plus more for drizzling

Juice of 2 lemons

2 tablespoons tahini

¼ teaspoon ground cumin

2 tablespoons water

Salt

Freshly ground black pepper

1 scallion, finely sliced

Halved cherry tomatoes, sugar snap peas, zucchini sticks, carrot sticks, red pepper strips, sliced radishes, blanched green beans, and cucumbers, for serving

1. In a small saucepan of boiling salted water, cook the garlic until softened, about 8 minutes. Let cool slightly and squeeze the garlic cloves from their skins.

2. In a food processor or a blender, combine the avocados, chickpeas, oil, lemon juice, tahini, cumin, blanched garlic, and water until creamy; season with salt and pepper and transfer to a bowl.

3. To serve, drizzle with olive oil and top with the scallion. Season with pepper and serve with the vegetables for dipping.

---

Ingredient Tip: Tahini is a sesame seed paste that comes in a jar. It can be found at most major supermarkets and will keep in the refrigerator for months. Tahini has more protein than milk and most nuts and is a good source of vitamin B, vitamin E, iron, and calcium.

# Cream Cheese & Cheddar Stuffed Jalapeño Poppers

**GLUTEN-FREE, VEGAN**
MAKES 12 / PREP TIME: 10 MINUTES / COOK TIME: 15 MINUTES

You can bake these poppers instead of frying. Just preheat the oven to 425°F and lightly grease a baking sheet with oil. Bake the stuffed and coated jalapeños, turning halfway through, until crunchy and golden, about 20 minutes.

**12 jalapeños**

**2 cups distilled white vinegar**

**2 tablespoons salt**

**2 teaspoons sugar**

**1 cup water**

**1 cup dairy-free shredded Cheddar cheese**

**½ cup homemade Cream Cheese or store-bought dairy-free cream cheese**

**1 teaspoon garlic powder**

**½ teaspoon onion powder**

**½ teaspoon paprika**

**½ teaspoon cornstarch**

**Neutral-flavored oil, for frying**

**¾ cup bread crumbs**

**4 large eggs or egg substitute (see tip)**

1. Cut a lengthwise slit from stem to bottom of each jalapeño. Make a crosswise incision at stem end and open enough to

remove the seeds.

2. In a medium saucepan over medium-high heat, bring the vinegar, salt, sugar, and water to a boil; cook until salt and sugar have dissolved. Remove from the heat, add the jalapeños, and let it sit until the jalapeños are softened, about 5 minutes. Drain and pat dry.

3. In a food processor, pulse together the Cheddar cheese, cream cheese, garlic powder, onion powder, paprika, and cornstarch until combined. Fill each jalapeño halfway with about 2 tablespoons of the cheese mixture, pressing to seal.

4. Fill a large pot with about 1 inch of oil and heat over medium heat until a thermometer registers 325°F.

5. Place the bread crumbs in one shallow bowl. In another shallow bowl, beat the eggs. Dip each jalapeño into the eggs, then coat with the bread crumbs; repeat and place on a parchment-lined baking sheet. Repeat with the remaining jalapeños.

6. Fry the jalapeños, turning occasionally and returning the oil to 325°F between batches, until golden brown and the cheese is melted, 3 to 5 minutes. Remove with a slotted spoon and drain on paper towels.

# Tortilla Chips with Chipotle Cheese Fondue

EGG-FREE, GLUTEN-FREE, ONE-POT, VEGAN
MAKES 2 CUPS / PREP TIME: 4 MINUTES / COOK TIME: 8 MINUTES

This cheesy fondue comes together in just minutes and reminds me of the jarred queso dip you find in the chip aisle of the supermarket. If you prefer using your microwave, go ahead and place the cheese fondue in a microwavable bowl, cover, and cook on high, stirring occasionally, until heated through.

**1 batch Cheese Sauce**

**2 tablespoons chopped chipotle peppers in adobo sauce**

**2 teaspoons chili powder**

**1 teaspoon chipotle powder**

**Salt**

**Tortilla chips, for serving**

In a saucepan over medium-low heat, stir together the cheese sauce, chipotle peppers in adobo sauce, chili powder, and chipotle powder; cook until warmed through, about 8 minutes. Add water, if necessary, 1 tablespoon at a time, until creamy; season with salt. Serve with tortilla chips.

Time-saving Tip: You can make this cheese fondue ahead of time—just stir together the ingredients, cover, and refrigerate until ready to heat and eat.

# Double-Baked Sour Cream & Chive Potatoes

5-INGREDIENT, EGG-FREE, FAMILY-FRIENDLY, GLUTEN-FREE, MAKE-AHEAD, ONE-POT, VEGAN

SERVES 4 / PREP TIME: 5 MINUTES / COOK TIME: 25 MINUTES

This old-school recipe brings back childhood memories for me. My mom always made this dish as a side for dinner alongside skillet steak, but I also love these stuffed potatoes as an easy afternoon snack. I wanted to dive into this nostalgic recipe and update it to be dairy-free.

**4 russet potatoes, scrubbed**

**½ cup homemade Sour Cream or store-bought dairy-free sour cream**

**¼ cup homemade Butter or store-bought dairy-free butter**

**2 tablespoons finely chopped fresh chives**

**Salt**

**Freshly ground black pepper**

**Dairy-free shredded Cheddar, for topping**

1. Preheat the oven to 425°F.

2. Using a fork, prick the potatoes all over and microwave on high until tender, about 8 to 10 minutes.

3. Cut each potato in half lengthwise. Leaving a ¼-inch thick potato shell, scoop the cooked potato flesh into a medium bowl. Add the sour cream, butter, and chives and mash well; season with salt and pepper.

4. Spoon the potato mixture back into the shells, top with Cheddar cheese, and place on a foil-lined baking sheet; bake until warmed through and the cheese is melted, about 15 minutes.

---

Time-saving Tip: You can bake the potatoes and assemble them ahead of time, then when you're ready to eat, just sprinkle with cheese and bake until hot and the cheese is melted.

# Three-Cheese Garlic Bread

EGG-FREE, FAMILY-FRIENDLY, VEGAN
SERVES 4 / PREP TIME: 10 MINUTES / COOK TIME: 15 MINUTES

This Italian American side dish is a classic—and this recipe balances garlic buttery goodness with rich, creamy cheesiness. I love to serve this garlic bread on its own as a snack or appetizer or alongside chicken Parmesan or even a big bowl of spaghetti.

**1 cup dairy-free shredded mozzarella-style cheese**

**½ cup homemade Grated Parmesan or store-bought dairy-free grated Parmesan**

**¼ cup homemade Ricotta or store-bought dairy-free ricotta**

**1 garlic clove, finely chopped**

**¼ cup finely chopped parsley**

**4 tablespoons homemade Butter or store-bought dairy-free butter, at room temperature**

**1 teaspoon salt**

**1 baguette, halved lengthwise and crosswise**

1. Preheat the oven to 400°F and line a baking sheet with foil.

2. In a small bowl, combine the mozzarella, Parmesan, ricotta, garlic, parsley, butter, and salt.

3. Place the baguette on the prepared baking sheet, cut-side up, and evenly spread on the cheese mixture; bake until golden, about 15 minutes.

Substitution Tip: **Gluten-free guests? Swap in a store-bought gluten-free baguette. If you don't have a baguette handy, try using separated hot dog buns in place of the baguette.**

# Bacon–Brussels Sprouts Hash

EGG-FREE, FAMILY-FRIENDLY, GLUTEN-FREE, NUT-FREE, ONE-POT
SERVES 4 TO 6 / PREP TIME: 8 MINUTES / COOK TIME: 20 MINUTES

My whole family has become addicted to this quick Brussels sprouts hash with its salty bacon, sweetened just a touch with caramel-like dates. You can serve this recipe as a side for breakfast, lunch, or dinner.

**2 russet potatoes**

**2 tablespoons olive oil**

**Salt**

**Freshly ground black pepper**

**4 slices slab bacon, chopped**

**1 pound Brussels sprouts, ends trimmed and halved**

**7 Medjool dates, pitted and chopped**

**1 tablespoon apple cider vinegar**

1. Using a fork, prick the potatoes all over and microwave on high until just tender, flipping once, about 8 minutes total; peel and cut into ½-inch pieces.

2. Preheat the oven to 425°F.

3. In a large skillet, heat the oil over medium-high heat until almost smoking. Add the potatoes and cook, undisturbed, until a crust forms, about 3 minutes; toss, shaking the pan, and cook until golden all over. Season generously with salt and pepper; drain on a paper towel–lined plate.

4. Wipe out the skillet with a paper towel, add the bacon, and cook

over medium heat until crispy, about 7 minutes; drain on paper towels, leaving about 2 tablespoons bacon grease in the pan.

5. Add the Brussels sprouts to the skillet, cut-side down; cook until tender and golden.

6. Add the dates, vinegar, and cooked bacon; season with salt and pepper and cook for 2 minutes. To serve, place some of the potato hash on plates and spoon over the Brussels sprouts and drippings.

---

Substitution Tip: If you don't have dates, just leave them out or swap in another dried fruit, such as cranberries, raisins, or chopped apricots.

# Cinnamon-Raisin Bread Breakfast Sausage Stuffing

EGG-FREE, FAMILY-FRIENDLY, NUT-FREE
SERVES 8 / PREP TIME: 5 MINUTES / COOK TIME: 25 MINUTES

I like to use comforting breakfast staples like cinnamon-raisin bread and breakfast sausage for my easy stuffing, which has long been a family favorite for the holidays. It's a totally different take on stuffing. You can also speed up the recipe by skipping toasting the bread for stuffing. Instead, use 8 cups of store-bought unseasoned stuffing cubes.

**12 slices cinnamon-raisin bread, cut into 1-inch cubes**

**1 pound precooked breakfast sausage, chopped**

**4 tablespoons homemade Butter or store-bought dairy-free butter, divided**

**1 onion, chopped**

**1 celery stalk, chopped**

**2 garlic cloves, finely chopped**

**1 tablespoon chopped fresh sage**

**Salt**

**Freshly ground black pepper**

**1 cup chicken broth**

1. Preheat the oven to 325°F.
2. Place the bread cubes in a single layer on 2 baking sheets; bake until lightly toasted, about 5 minutes. Transfer the bread to

a large bowl and add the precooked sausage. Increase the oven temperature to 425°F.

3. Heat 2 tablespoons of butter in a skillet; add the onion, celery, garlic, and sage and cook over medium-high heat, stirring occasionally, until softened, about 5 minutes; season with salt and pepper.

4. Add the onion and celery mixture to the bread mixture along with the chicken broth and toss.

5. Transfer the stuffing mixture to a greased 11-by-7-by-2-inch baking dish and dot the top with the remaining 2 tablespoons of butter.

6. Cover with foil and bake for 15 minutes, then uncover and bake until golden, about 10 minutes more.

Substitution Tip: If you have extra time, use your favorite fresh breakfast sausage instead of precooked. To prepare, remove the casings and cook the sausage in a large skillet over medium-high heat, breaking up the meat, until browned, about 5 minutes.

# Chinese-Style Honey-Mustard Chicken Wings

EGG-FREE, FAMILY-FRIENDLY, MAKE-AHEAD
SERVES 4 / PREP TIME: 8 MINUTES / COOK TIME: 20 MINUTES

This recipe combines the classic flavors of honey mustard with soy sauce and rice wine vinegar, which gives the wings a surprising umami taste. This twist on classic chicken wings is a huge hit with my kids and guests. I love to make this for a barbecue or potluck gathering.

**2 pounds chicken wings, patted dry**

**2 tablespoons olive oil**

**Salt**

**Freshly ground black pepper**

**½ cup Dijon mustard**

**¼ cup honey**

**¼ cup Egg-Free Mayonnaise or store-bought mayonnaise**

**1 tablespoon rice wine vinegar**

**2 teaspoons soy sauce**

**¼ teaspoon ground turmeric**

1. Preheat the oven to 425°F and line a baking sheet with foil.
2. Place the wings on the prepared baking sheet, drizzle with the oil, and season generously with salt and pepper; toss to coat and arrange the wings in a single layer. Roast, until cooked

through and golden, turning the wings halfway, about 20 minutes total.

3. In a small saucepan, whisk together the mustard, honey, mayonnaise, vinegar, soy sauce, and turmeric; bring to a boil over medium-high heat, stirring, then remove from the heat and season with salt and pepper. Pour over the roasted wings and toss to coat.

---

Substitution Tip: If you don't have rice wine vinegar on hand, swap in white wine vinegar or apple cider vinegar.

# Ranch Chicken Nuggets

FAMILY-FRIENDLY, NUT-FREE

SERVES 4 / PREP TIME: 10 MINUTES / COOK TIME: 20 MINUTES

This is my favorite riff on the classic chicken cordon bleu. I roll ham around chicken and instead of using Gruyère cheese, I swap in ranch dressing for a creamy surprise inside and to keep the chicken perfectly moist and juicy.

½ **cup all-purpose flour**

**2 large eggs or egg substitute (see tip), beaten with 1 tablespoon water**

**1 cup bread crumbs**

¾ **teaspoon salt**

¼ **teaspoon pepper**

**6 slices deli ham (about ½ pound), cut lengthwise into 1-inch-wide strips**

½ **cup homemade Ranch Dressing or store-bought dairy-free ranch dressing**

**2 large boneless, skinless chicken breasts (about 1 pound), cut into 1-inch-wide pieces**

**Cooking spray**

1. Preheat the oven to 350°F. Set two wire racks over two baking sheets and spray with cooking spray.

2. Place the flour on a plate and the egg and water mixture in a shallow bowl. Combine the bread crumbs, salt, and pepper on another plate.

3. Place the ham strips on a work surface and put a dollop of ranch dressing at the end of each strip. Top with a piece of chicken and roll up to enclose.

4. Lightly coat each rolled-up chicken and ham piece with the flour, then egg, then bread crumbs. Place seam-side down, on the wire racks. Lightly spray the nuggets with cooking spray. Bake until crisp and cooked through, about 20 minutes.

**Grilled Vegetable Pizza with Herbed Goat Cheese**

# CHAPTER SIX

# Vegetarian Mains

Sicilian Deep-Dish Pizza

Grilled Vegetable Pizza with Herbed Goat Cheese

Falafel Taco with Citrus Crema

Veggie Ranchero Bowls

Stovetop Mac & Cheese

Eggplant Teriyaki

Santa Fe Sweet Potato & Corn Chili

Spaghetti with Creamy Ricotta Pesto Sauce

Brussels Sprouts Penne Carbonara

Beet-Walnut Veggie Burger with Cheddar Cheese

Sesame Noodles with Broccoli

Quinoa Tabbouleh with Smoky Tahini Dressing

Black Bean–Avocado Burritos

Korean Barbecue–Style Veggie Bowl

Cauliflower Steaks with Whipped Garlic Ricotta

# Sicilian Deep-Dish Pizza

**EGG-FREE, FAMILY-FRIENDLY, GOOD FOR LEFTOVERS**
**MAKES 2 (9-INCH) PIZZAS / PREP TIME: 5 MINUTES / COOK TIME: 20 MINUTES**

I don't always have the patience—or the time—to make and proof my own dough. My secret to this speedy pizza is using premade dough. You can definitely make your own pizza dough, just make sure to allow enough time for kneading and letting it rise at least once at room temperature until it doubles in size, which can take about 90 minutes. Make this pizza your own with fun toppings. My kids love to pick the ingredients and top the pizzas themselves.

**6 tablespoons olive oil**

**All-purpose flour, for dusting**

**1½ pounds store-bought pizza dough, at room temperature and halved**

**1 cup store-bought dairy-free canned pizza sauce**

**3 cups dairy-free shredded mozzarella cheese**

**¼ cup homemade Grated Parmesan or store-bought dairy-free grated Parmesan**

**Various toppings, such as pepperoni, cooked sausage crumbles, thinly sliced red onion, bell pepper, or mushrooms**

1. Preheat the oven to 400°F. Divide the olive oil to grease two 9-inch round cake pans.

2. On a piece of parchment paper lightly dusted with flour, roll out each half of the dough to a 9-inch round and transfer to the prepared pans.

3. Spread half of the sauce over each dough round and top with the mozzarella, Parmesan, and any other toppings. Bake until

golden and bubbling, about 20 minutes. Let the pizza cool slightly before serving.

---

Cooking Tip: The trick to making sure the crust gets nice and crunchy is to not use too much pizza sauce or pile on too many toppings. This gives the crust room to grow and bake.

# Grilled Vegetable Pizza with Herbed Goat Cheese

EGG-FREE, FAMILY-FRIENDLY, VEGAN
MAKES 2 (8½-INCH) PIZZAS / PREP TIME: 10 MINUTES / COOK TIME: 13 MINUTES

Come summertime, I love to spend time outside gardening and, of course, grilling, even when it comes to making pizza. The best part? There is almost zero cleanup. This grilled pizza is a family favorite, and I love to include my kids in making and topping it. If you have a pizza peel (paddle), use that instead of the inverted baking sheet.

½ small eggplant, sliced crosswise into ½-inch rounds

1 zucchini, sliced crosswise into ½-inch rounds

2 plum tomatoes, sliced crosswise into ½-inch rounds

4 ounces (125 grams) asparagus, ends trimmed and cut into 3-inch pieces

Olive oil, for brushing

Salt

Freshly ground black pepper

1 pound store-bought dairy-free pizza dough, at room temperature and halved

6 tablespoons store-bought dairy-free canned pizza sauce

1 batch homemade Herbed Goat Cheese or store-bought dairy-free herbed goat cheese, for topping

1. Preheat a grill or grill pan to medium-high heat.

2. Brush the eggplant, zucchini, tomatoes, and asparagus with olive oil; season with salt and pepper. Grill, turning once, until tender and slightly charred, about 5 minutes.

3. On a lightly oiled inverted baking sheet, roll out 1 piece of the pizza dough to make a round about ¼ inch thick; brush with olive oil. Repeat with the remaining dough.

4. Shimmy each piece of pizza dough off the baking sheet and onto the grill; cook with the grill cover down (if you're using a grill pan, tent with aluminum foil) until the crust holds its shape and grill marks appear, about 3 minutes.

5. Using a heatproof spatula, flip each crust over onto the coolest part of the grill. Spread 3 tablespoons of the sauce over each pizza crust, leaving a ½-inch border of plain crust. Top each with half of the grilled vegetables and cook with the grill cover down (or aluminum tent) until the crust is golden, 3 to 5 minutes.

6. Remove the pizzas from the grill and top each with dollops of goat cheese.

Ingredient Tip: Want to make your own pizza sauce? Just stir together 6 tablespoons strained tomatoes, a drizzle of oil, and a pinch each of sugar, salt, pepper, and dried oregano.

# Falafel Taco with Citrus Crema

EGG-FREE, FAMILY-FRIENDLY, GLUTEN-FREE, MAKE-AHEAD, VEGAN
SERVES 4 / PREP TIME: 10 MINUTES / COOK TIME: 15 MINUTES

I love playing around with cuisines from around the world. In this recipe, I was inspired by ingredients and classic dishes from the Middle East and Mexico. If you don't have chickpea flour in your pantry, you can substitute all-purpose flour. You can fry up the falafel and keep refrigerated for up to 3 days. Reheat in a toaster oven until warmed through.

**FOR THE CREMA**

¾ cup homemade Sour Cream or store-bought dairy-free sour cream

¼ cup orange juice

2 tablespoons finely chopped cilantro or parsley

2 teaspoons lime juice

1 teaspoon ground cumin

1 teaspoon salt

**FOR THE FALAFEL TACO**

2 (19-ounce) cans of chickpeas, rinsed, drained, and patted dry

4 garlic cloves, smashed

½ onion, coarsely chopped

¼ cup chickpea flour

1 teaspoon salt

1 teaspoon baking powder

½ teaspoon chili powder

¼ teaspoon pepper

Zest of ½ an orange

Zest of ½ a lime

2 teaspoons olive oil

1 tablespoon water

Neutral-flavored oil, for frying

Corn tortillas, warmed

Chopped tomato, cucumber, onion, and avocado, for serving

### TO MAKE THE CREMA

In a small bowl, whisk together the sour cream with the orange juice, cilantro, lime juice, cumin, and salt; cover and refrigerate.

### TO MAKE THE FALAFEL TACOS

1. In the bowl of a food processor, pulse together the chickpeas, garlic, onion, flour, salt, baking powder, chili powder, pepper, orange zest, lime zest, olive oil, and water until coarsely puréed. Using a 1½-inch scoop or a heaping tablespoon, form the falafel mixture into balls.

2. In a deep pot, heat 3 inches of oil to 375°. Working in batches, fry the falafel until golden brown, about 5 minutes; drain on paper towels and repeat.

3. Serve the falafel in the warmed tortillas with the crema, tomato, cucumber, onion, and avocado.

---

Time-saving Tip: You can make the crema ahead of time and keep it refrigerated for up to 3 days. Bring to room temperature before serving and if needed, thin it with another 1 to 2 tablespoons of water.

# Veggie Ranchero Bowls

EGG-FREE, NUT-FREE, VEGAN
MAKES 6 / PREP TIME: 10 MINUTES / COOK TIME: 20 MINUTES

These fun tortilla bowls are easy to make using an inverted muffin pan. To soften the tortillas, just stack them on a microwave-safe plate, cover and microwave until softened, about 30 seconds on high. Interesting fact: Chile powder is dried chile ground into powder, while chili powder is a mix of different spices including ground chile, cumin, peppercorn, and salt.

6 (6-inch) flour tortillas, softened

2 tablespoons olive oil

2 zucchini, cut into thin rounds

1 ear corn, kernels sliced from cob

1 red onion, chopped

1 red bell pepper, seeded and chopped

1 small jalapeño, seeded and chopped

2 garlic cloves, smashed

2 teaspoons chile powder

1 teaspoon cumin powder

Salt

1 (15-ounce) can crushed tomatoes

Chopped avocado, dairy-free shredded Cheddar, store-bought salsa, cilantro, and lime wedges, for serving

1. Preheat the oven to 375°F. Invert a muffin pan and lightly grease the back of six muffin cups with cooking spray.

2. Place the softened tortillas over the greased muffin cups to cover. Bake until golden and crisp, about 15 minutes. Let cool slightly, then remove the taco bowls from the pan and invert onto a wire rack to cool completely.

3. In a large skillet, heat the oil over medium-high heat. Add the zucchini, corn, onion, bell pepper, jalapeño, garlic, chile powder, cumin powder, and salt to taste; cook until softened.

4. Stir in the tomatoes and simmer until warmed through, about 5 minutes; divide among the tortilla bowls and serve with the toppings.

Time-saving Tip: **No time to bake the bowls? Go ahead and serve the vegetable filling in warmed-up tortillas as tacos.**

# Stovetop Mac & Cheese

5-INGREDIENT, EGG-FREE, FAMILY-FRIENDLY, VEGAN
SERVES 4 TO 6 / PREP TIME: 3 MINUTES / COOK TIME: 15 MINUTES

This is easily everyone's favorite dinner. Macaroni and cheese is the ultimate comfort food, so I had to make a dairy-free version for this cookbook. The butternut squash adds just a touch of sweetness and extra creaminess to the cheese sauce.

**3 cups (12 ounces) elbow macaroni pasta**

**1½ cups Cheese Sauce, at room temperature**

**½ cup canned butternut squash purée**

**Salt**

1. In a large saucepan of boiling salted water, cook the macaroni until al dente; drain.

2. Meanwhile, heat the cheese sauce over medium-low heat and whisk in the butternut squash purée until combined. Cook until warmed through, about 8 minutes; season with salt. Place the sauce in a large serving bowl and stir in the cooked macaroni to coat.

Ingredient Tip: For a baked version with some crunch, transfer the cooked mac and cheese to an oven-safe dish, then combine ½ cup homemade Grated Parmesan or store-bought dairy-free grated Parmesan and ¼ cup bread crumbs in a small bowl and sprinkle it over the top; broil for 2 minutes or until golden.

# Eggplant Teriyaki

**EGG-FREE, NUT-FREE, VEGAN**
SERVES 4 / PREP TIME: 5 MINUTES / COOK TIME: 25 MINUTES

I love to serve this Eggplant Teriyaki with coconut rice. For an easy coconut rice, put 1 cup long-grain white rice, 1½ cups coconut milk, and 2 chopped scallions in a large saucepan and bring to a boil. Reduce the heat to low, cover, and cook until all the liquid is absorbed and the rice is tender, about 25 minutes; fluff with a fork and season with salt. The teriyaki sauce can be made ahead of time and refrigerated for up to 1 month.

**¼ cup tamari or soy sauce**

**2 tablespoons mirin**

**2 tablespoons vegetable broth or water**

**2 tablespoons brown sugar**

**3 tablespoons olive oil (1 tablespoon used first, then 2 tablespoons used later)**

**1½ teaspoons rice wine vinegar or apple cider vinegar**

**2 garlic cloves, chopped**

**1 teaspoon freshly grated ginger**

**Zest and juice of ½ orange**

**1½ teaspoons cornstarch dissolved in 1 tablespoon water**

**3 medium eggplant, ends trimmed and halved lengthwise**

**Sesame seeds, for serving (optional)**

1. Add the tamari, mirin, broth, sugar, 1 tablespoon of oil, vinegar, garlic, ginger, orange zest, and orange juice to a blender; process until smooth. Transfer to a small saucepan and bring to

a boil. Reduce the heat to medium-low and simmer until slightly thickened, about 8 minutes.

2. Stir in the cornstarch slurry and return to a boil. Cook, stirring, until glossy, about 2 minutes.

3. Score the flesh of the eggplant in a crisscross pattern, making sure not to cut all the way through. Generously brush the eggplant on the crisscross side with the teriyaki sauce.

4. In a large skillet, heat the remaining 2 tablespoons of oil over medium heat. Working in batches if necessary, place the eggplant in the skillet, crisscross-side down, brush on more teriyaki sauce, and cook uncovered and turning once, until softened and caramelized, about 8 minutes. Repeat with the remaining eggplant and teriyaki sauce. To serve, sprinkle with sesame seeds (if using).

---

Substitution Tips: If you're pressed for time, swap in store-bought gluten-free teriyaki sauce, and if you don't have mirin, a Japanese sweet rice wine, on hand, substitute 1 tablespoon sugar and ¼ cup of white wine or dry sherry.

# Santa Fe Sweet Potato & Corn Chili

**EGG-FREE, FAMILY-FRIENDLY, GLUTEN-FREE, VEGAN**
SERVES 4 / PREP TIME: 7 MINUTES / COOK TIME: 23 MINUTES

This is one of my favorite chili recipes. I threw in satisfying sweet potato and sweet corn to make this chili a hearty meal. If you can't find fire-roasted diced tomatoes at your supermarket, use plain diced tomatoes instead.

2 tablespoons olive oil

2 garlic cloves, finely chopped

1 yellow onion, chopped

2 yellow bell peppers, seeded and chopped

2 ears corn, kernels removed, about 2 cups

2 sweet potatoes, peeled and cut into ½-inch pieces

1½ tablespoons chili powder

1 teaspoon ground cumin

1 teaspoon dried oregano

1 teaspoon unsweetened cocoa powder

1 teaspoon salt

1 (28-ounce) can fire-roasted diced tomatoes

1 cup vegetable broth or water

1 (15-ounce) can black beans, rinsed and drained

Homemade Sour Cream or store-bought dairy-free sour cream, dairy-free shredded Cheddar, sliced scallions, sliced radishes, and tortilla chips, for topping

1. In a medium pot, heat the oil over medium-high heat. Add the garlic, onion, bell peppers, corn, sweet potatoes, chili powder, cumin, oregano, cocoa powder, and salt; cook, stirring, until softened, about 8 minutes.

2. Add the tomatoes, broth, and beans; bring to a boil, then reduce the heat to low and simmer until slightly reduced and warmed through, about 15 minutes. Season with salt and serve with the toppings.

---

Cooking Tip: If you want to make this chili in a slow cooker, add all ingredients except the beans to your slow cooker and cook for 4 to 5 hours on high until the sweet potatoes are tender. Then add the beans and let the flavors blend for 1 to 2 hours on the low setting. Serve with the toppings.

# Spaghetti with Creamy Ricotta Pesto Sauce

EGG-FREE, FAMILY-FRIENDLY, VEGAN

SERVES 4 / PREP TIME: 10 MINUTES / COOK TIME: 8 MINUTES

Unlike its classic bright green counterpart, this spaghetti is sauced with a white rich and creamy ricotta-based pesto. While a traditional pesto is made with pine nuts, this creamier version has finely chopped walnuts to give it a nuttier flavor and offset some of the richness from the cheese.

**1 pound spaghetti**

**1 cup homemade Ricotta or store-bought dairy-free ricotta**

**½ cup homemade Grated Parmesan or store-bought dairy-free grated Parmesan, plus more for topping**

**½ cup roasted walnuts, finely chopped**

**1 garlic clove, finely chopped**

**2 teaspoons finely chopped parsley**

**Zest of 1 lemon**

**¼ cup olive oil**

**Salt**

**Freshly ground black pepper**

1. Cook the spaghetti in a large pot of boiling salted water until al dente, about 8 minutes; reserve 1 cup of the cooking water and drain.

2. Meanwhile, in the bowl of a food processor, pulse together the ricotta, Parmesan, walnuts, garlic, parsley, and lemon zest. With

the motor running, slowly stream in the oil; season with salt and pepper.

3. Place the pesto in a large bowl and stir in the cooked spaghetti, adding enough reserved cooking water, 2 tablespoons at a time, to make the sauce thinner to cling to the pasta. Divide the spaghetti among bowls and top with Parmesan.

---

Time-saving Tip: If you want to save some time, you can purchase store-bought pesto sauce and use ¼ cup pesto sauce, 2 cups of ricotta, and the 1 cup reserved pasta water. Add all 3 ingredients to a small pan over medium-high heat and stir until well combined before tossing it with the pasta.

# Brussels Sprouts Penne Carbonara

FAMILY-FRIENDLY, VEGETARIAN
SERVES 4 / PREP TIME: 10 MINUTES / COOK TIME: 12 MINUTES

Carbonara is a traditional Roman pasta sauce typically made with *guanciale* (cured pork), eggs, pecorino cheese, and lots of black pepper. Here, I've swapped in Brussels sprouts, shiitake mushrooms, and Parmesan to make a vegetarian version with the same light feel. When you stir the hot pasta into the egg mixture, the residual heat cooks the eggs to a safe temperature and makes a delicious sauce.

1 pound penne pasta

2 tablespoons olive oil

8 ounces shredded Brussels sprouts

8 ounces sliced shiitake mushrooms

1 garlic clove, smashed

2 large eggs or egg substitute (see tip), at room temperature

**Freshly ground black pepper**

**Salt**

**¼ cup homemade Grated Parmesan or store-bought dairy-free grated Parmesan**

1. Cook the pasta in a large pot of boiling salted water until al dente, about 12 minutes; reserve 1 cup of the cooking water and drain.

2. Meanwhile, heat the oil in a large skillet over medium-high heat

and cook the Brussels sprouts, mushrooms, and garlic, stirring occasionally, until browned, about 5 minutes.

3. In a large serving bowl, whisk together the eggs and season with plenty of pepper. Add the drained pasta and Brussels sprouts mixture; toss to combine, adding a little pasta cooking water, 1 tablespoon at a time, to loosen if needed, and season with salt, if needed. Serve with the Parmesan sprinkled on top.

---

Cooking Tip: To shred the Brussels sprouts, you can use a mandoline for uniform pieces or just chop them with a large knife. Make sure to always use a safety guard when using a mandoline to protect your fingers.

# Beet-Walnut Veggie Burger with Cheddar Cheese

**FAMILY-FRIENDLY, MAKE-AHEAD**
MAKES 8 / PREP TIME: 5 MINUTES / COOK TIME: 25 MINUTES

I love a good veggie burger that actually tastes like vegetables rather than trying to imitate meat. If I have extra time, I refrigerate the shaped veggie patties for 30 minutes to let them set. You can also make these patties ahead of time and freeze them.

1 cup finely shredded carrots

1 cup finely shredded cabbage

1 cup finely shredded raw beets

1 cup cooked quinoa

½ cup bread crumbs

½ cup finely chopped walnuts

1 small onion, finely chopped

2 tablespoons olive oil

1 teaspoon apple cider vinegar

2 large eggs or egg substitute (see tip)

¼ cup chopped parsley

½ teaspoon salt

½ teaspoon pepper

8 burger buns, toasted, for serving (optional)

8 slices dairy-free Cheddar cheese

Romaine lettuce, for serving

Tomato, sliced, for serving

**Avocado, sliced, for serving**

1. Preheat the oven to 350°F.

2. In a large bowl, combine the carrots, cabbage, beets, quinoa, bread crumbs, walnuts, onion, oil, vinegar, eggs, parsley, salt, and pepper; shape into 8 burgers.

3. Place the burgers on a parchment-lined baking sheet and bake until lightly browned and heated through, about 25 minutes. Place the burger on a bun bottom (if using). Assemble the rest of the burger by adding the cheese, romaine, tomato, avocado, and a bun top.

Substitution Tip: If you don't want to use traditional burger buns, or want a lower-carb option, swap in Boston lettuce or iceberg lettuce leaves.

# Sesame Noodles with Broccoli

CALCIUM-RICH, EGG-FREE, VEGAN
SERVES 4 / PREP TIME: 8 MINUTES / COOK TIME: 22 MINUTES

The broccoli in this dish—blended until smooth—adds a sweet, earthy element to the more traditional peanut butter–based sesame dressing. If you want more protein, just toss in about ½ pound of firm tofu cut into ½-inch cubes.

1 pound linguine

¼ pound broccoli florets, blanched for 1 minute and drained

¼ cup cashews, soaked in hot water for 15 minutes and drained

2 garlic cloves, divided

½ cup cilantro or parsley leaves

2 tablespoons neutral-flavored oil

2 tablespoons plus ⅓ cup water (2 tablespoons used first, ⅓ cup used later)

Salt

3 tablespoons natural unsalted peanut butter

2 tablespoons sesame oil

2 tablespoons tamari or soy sauce

1 tablespoon rice wine vinegar or white wine vinegar

2 teaspoons sugar

¼ teaspoon crushed red pepper or more to taste

2 teaspoons grated ginger

1. Cook the pasta in a large pot of boiling salted water until al dente, 8 to 10 minutes; drain and rinse with cold water.

2. Place the broccoli, cashews, 1 garlic clove, and cilantro in a blender; process to finely chop and, with the motor running, drizzle in the oil. Drizzle in 2 tablespoons of water and blend until smooth, adding more water, 1 tablespoon at a time, if necessary; season with salt. Set aside.

3. Place the peanut butter, sesame oil, tamari, vinegar, sugar, crushed red pepper, ginger, and remaining 1 garlic clove in a blender; process to combine. With the motor running, drizzle in the remaining ⅓ cup of water and blend until smooth, adding more water, 1 tablespoon at a time, if necessary.

4. Toss the cooked linguine noodles with the broccoli mixture and sesame sauce to coat evenly.

Substitution Tip: To make this recipe gluten-free, swap in buckwheat noodles or rice noodles for the linguine.

# Quinoa Tabbouleh with Smoky Tahini Dressing

CALCIUM-RICH, EGG-FREE, GLUTEN-FREE, MAKE-AHEAD, NUT-FREE, VEGAN
SERVES 4 / PREP TIME: 8 MINUTES / COOK TIME: 12 MINUTES

I love classic tabbouleh salad, but, for a twist, I swap in quinoa for the bulgur and add a creamy smoky tahini dressing. Quinoa has a lot of nutritional benefits, being a great source of fiber, iron, vitamin B6, and magnesium. The tabbouleh salad can be refrigerated for up to 1 day before serving.

### FOR THE TABBOULEH

1 cup quinoa

¼ teaspoon salt

1¾ cups water

10 cherry tomatoes, halved

1 seedless cucumber, peeled and cut into ½-inch pieces

2 tablespoons chopped flat-leaf parsley

2 tablespoons chopped mint

Salt

Freshly ground black pepper

### FOR THE DRESSING

½ cup tahini

2 tablespoons lemon juice

1 garlic clove

¾ teaspoon ground smoked paprika

½ teaspoon ground cumin

½ teaspoon salt

½ cup water

**TO MAKE THE TABBOULEH**

1. In a small saucepan, bring the quinoa, salt, and water to a boil; reduce the heat to low and simmer, covered, until the liquid is absorbed, about 12 minutes. Fluff with a fork to combine and put in a large bowl.

2. Add the tomatoes, cucumber, parsley, and mint. Season with salt and pepper; toss well.

**TO MAKE THE DRESSING**

In a blender, combine the tahini, lemon juice, garlic, paprika, cumin, salt, and water until creamy; add to the tabbouleh and toss to coat.

# Black Bean–Avocado Burritos

**EGG-FREE, FAMILY-FRIENDLY, NUT-FREE, VEGAN**
SERVES 4 / PREP TIME: 10 MINUTES / COOK TIME: 20 MINUTES

This is a simple yet satisfying main dish that's easy to assemble on a weeknight. If you prefer, you can turn this into a burrito bowl—just omit the flour tortillas and stack the ingredients into bowls.

1 cup short-grain white rice

¼ teaspoon salt

1¾ cups water

2 tablespoons olive oil

1 onion, thinly sliced

1 bell pepper, seeded and thinly sliced

2 (15-ounce) cans black beans, rinsed and drained

2 garlic cloves, finely chopped

Salt

Freshly ground black pepper

1 tablespoon fresh lime juice

1 jalapeño, seeded and finely chopped (optional)

4 (10-inch) flour tortillas

1 cup dairy-free shredded Cheddar cheese

2 avocados, sliced

1. In a small saucepan, bring the rice, salt, and water to a boil; reduce the heat to low and simmer, covered, until the liquid is absorbed, about 12 minutes. Fluff with a fork.

2. Heat the oil in a skillet over medium-high heat and add the onion and bell pepper; cook until softened, about 5 minutes.

3. Reduce the heat to medium-low and stir in the black beans and garlic; cook until heated through, about 3 minutes, and season with salt and pepper. Remove from the heat and stir in the cooked rice, lime juice, and jalapeño (if using).

4. Warm the tortillas in the microwave or in a dry skillet, then transfer to a clean, dry surface. Leaving space around the edges for rolling, top each tortilla with a quarter of the filling, cheese, and avocado slices. To roll up, fold the short sides in while rolling forward to seal in the filling. To serve, slice diagonally through the center.

Ingredient Tip: If you want to make this meal with meat, shredded chicken is delicious with black beans and works well with the creaminess of avocado. Cut 1 pound of chicken into strips and cook it in a large skillet over medium-high heat until cooked all the way through; 6 to 8 minutes. Season with salt and pepper and add it to your burritos.

# Korean Barbecue–Style Veggie Bowl

EGG-FREE, FAMILY-FRIENDLY, NUT-FREE, VEGAN
SERVES 4 / PREP TIME: 10 MINUTES / COOK TIME: 20 MINUTES

Korean barbecue is a personal favorite, and you know I love vegetables. Typically, Korean barbecue bowls have meat in them, but this vegan version is packed full of nutritious and delicious cooked vegetables. What I love about this veggie bowl is that it's versatile—I can use whatever vegetables I have sitting in my refrigerator crisper and it always tastes good.

**1 cup jasmine rice**

**3 tablespoons neutral-flavored oil (1 tablespoon used first, 2 tablespoons used later)**

**1½ cups water**

**Salt**

**2 garlic cloves, finely chopped**

**2 scallions, finely chopped**

**½ cup store-bought dairy-free barbecue sauce**

**¼ cup soy sauce**

**2 (15-ounce) cans chickpeas, rinsed and drained**

**2 zucchini, cut into thin rounds**

**1 red bell pepper, seeded and cut into thin strips**

**2 cups sugar snap peas, ends trimmed**

**1 cup coleslaw mix, for topping**

1. In a medium saucepan, bring the rice, 1 tablespoon of oil, water, and a pinch of salt to a boil; reduce the heat to low and simmer, covered, until the liquid is absorbed, about 12 minutes. Fluff with a fork.

2. Meanwhile, in a medium bowl, toss together the garlic, scallions, barbecue sauce, soy sauce, and chickpeas; toss to coat and let marinate until ready to use.

3. Heat the remaining 2 tablespoons of oil in a large skillet over medium-high heat and add the zucchini, bell pepper, and peas; cook, stirring frequently, until tender and golden, about 5 minutes, then season with salt and remove to a plate.

4. Add the marinated chickpeas to the same skillet and cook until warmed through and the sauce has thickened slightly, about 3 minutes; season with salt, if needed.

5. To serve, divide the rice evenly into 4 bowls, top with a quarter each of the zucchini mixture, barbecue chickpea mixture, and coleslaw mix for crunch.

---

Substitution Tip: In place of the jasmine rice, go ahead and use any kind of rice, couscous, or bulgur you have on hand.

# Cauliflower Steaks with Whipped Garlic Ricotta

**EGG-FREE, FAMILY-FRIENDLY, GLUTEN-FREE, VEGAN**
**SERVES 4 / PREP TIME: 10 MINUTES / COOK TIME: 20 MINUTES**

Cauliflower is a versatile ingredient because it does not have an overwhelming flavor on its own. You can make it taste like anything you want using spices and herbs. The whipped ricotta can be made up to 2 days ahead; just cover and refrigerate, then bring to room temperature before serving.

### FOR THE CAULIFLOWER STEAKS

**2 large heads of cauliflower, stems lightly trimmed**

**2 tablespoons olive oil, divided**

**Salt**

**Freshly ground black pepper**

### FOR THE WHIPPED GARLIC RICOTTA

**4 garlic cloves, with skins on**

**1 cup homemade Ricotta or store-bought dairy-free ricotta**

**2 tablespoons olive oil**

**1 teaspoon finely grated lemon zest**

**2 tablespoons lemon juice**

**2 tablespoons chopped parsley**

**Salt**

**Freshly ground black pepper**

## TO MAKE THE CAULIFLOWER STEAKS

1. Preheat the oven to 375° and cut four ¾-inch-thick center slices from each head of cauliflower to make steaks.

2. In a large skillet, heat 1 tablespoon of oil until shimmering. Working in batches, add all 4 cauliflower steaks and season with salt and pepper. Cook over medium heat, turning once, until lightly browned, about 3 minutes on each side; transfer to a rimmed baking sheet. Repeat with the remaining 1 tablespoon of oil and the other 4 cauliflower steaks.

3. Put the baking sheet in the oven and bake the cauliflower steaks until tender and browned, about 20 minutes.

## TO MAKE THE WHIPPED GARLIC RICOTTA

1. Place the garlic cloves in a microwave-safe bowl and cover; microwave on high until softened, about 1½ minutes. Let cool and remove the garlic from the skins.

2. In a food processor or blender, combine the ricotta, olive oil, lemon zest, lemon juice, and cooked garlic until smooth; stir in the parsley and season with salt and pepper. To serve, spoon ricotta mixture over the cauliflower steaks.

---

Ingredient Tip: As a side dish, make cauliflower rice with the leftover cauliflower. Place it in a food processor and pulse until the mixture resembles rice, then flavor with your favorite spices and add creaminess with homemade Butter or store-bought dairy-free butter.

**Poached Salmon with Dill Pickle Mayo**

# CHAPTER SEVEN

# Meats & Fish

Chicken Cordon Bleu with Fondue Dipping Sauce

Skillet Chicken Parmesan

Creamy Chicken-Vegetable Potpie

Buffalo Chicken Fingers with Sour Cream & Chive Dip

Sour Cream Mashed Potato–Stuffed Chicken

Marsala Chicken Pasta Bake

Turkey Sloppy Joe Pizza Pockets

Bacon-Wrapped Maple-Mustard Pork Tenderloin

Salsa Steak Tacos

Boursin-Style Cheese-Stuffed Burgers

Tex-Mex Meatloaf Pie

Crispy Fish Sticks with Sweet Relish Tartar Sauce

Fried Shrimp with Creamy Coleslaw

Spicy Chipotle Shrimp

Poached Salmon with Dill Pickle Mayo

# Chicken Cordon Bleu with Fondue Dipping Sauce

**EGG-FREE, FAMILY-FRIENDLY**
**SERVES 4 / PREP TIME: 10 MINUTES / COOK TIME: 16 MINUTES**

This seemingly sophisticated Swiss-inspired dish is surprisingly easy, even on a weeknight. The chicken stuffed with ham and cheese is satisfying on its own, but the quick fondue dip takes this dish over the top and makes it fun to eat.

**8 thin-sliced skinless, boneless chicken breast cutlets**

**12 slices store-bought dairy-free Swiss-style cheese, 4 slices torn into pieces**

**4 slices deli ham**

**½ cup all-purpose flour**

**1 teaspoon paprika**

**½ teaspoon salt**

**¼ teaspoon pepper**

**2 tablespoons olive oil**

**1½ cups Classic Party Fondue**

1. On a clean, dry work surface, form 4 "sandwiches" by layering 1 cutlet, 1 slice of cheese, 1 slice of ham, another slice of cheese, and a second chicken cutlet, then fasten the sandwiches in the center with a toothpick. Repeat with the remaining chicken, ham, and cheese.

2. On a plate, stir together the flour, paprika, salt, and pepper. Dredge a sandwich in the flour to coat both sides, shaking off

any excess. Repeat with the remaining sandwiches.

3. In a large skillet, heat the olive oil over medium-high heat and cook the chicken until cooked through and golden, turning once, about 6 minutes total. Serve with the fondue.

---

Substitution Tip: **Can't find dairy-free Swiss cheese? Swap in dairy-free provolone or smoked Gouda instead.**

# Skillet Chicken Parmesan

**EGG-FREE, FAMILY-FRIENDLY, ONE-POT**
**SERVES 4 / PREP TIME: 6 MINUTES / COOK TIME: 24 MINUTES**

This is a one-pot meal your family will want to eat over and over again. If you don't want to pound the chicken into thin, even pieces to speed up the cooking process, you can use store-bought, thin-sliced chicken breast cutlets instead.

**2 tablespoons olive oil**

**3 garlic cloves, smashed**

**½ cup all-purpose flour**

**4 boneless skinless chicken breasts, pounded thin**

**Salt**

**Freshly ground black pepper**

**1 cup long-grain white rice, rinsed in cold water and drained**

**1 (14.5-ounce) can chopped tomatoes**

**1 cup store-bought chicken broth or water**

**2 teaspoons salt**

**1 (8-ounce) can tomato sauce**

**6 basil leaves**

**¼ cup homemade Grated Parmesan or store-bought dairy-free grated Parmesan**

**1 cup shredded dairy-free mozzarella-style cheese**

1. In a large skillet, heat the oil over medium-high heat. Add the garlic and cook until golden, about 1 minute.

2. Put the flour on a plate. Season the chicken generously with salt

and pepper and lightly dredge both sides in the flour; add to the skillet and cook, turning once, until browned, about 4 minutes total. Transfer to a plate.

3. Add the rice, tomatoes, broth, and salt to the skillet; bring to a boil. Top with the cooked chicken, tomato sauce, basil, Parmesan, and mozzarella. Cover with a lid or foil, reduce the heat to low, and simmer until the rice is cooked, about 20 minutes.

---

Substitution Tip: **Swap turkey cutlets for the chicken if you prefer a more lean option.**

# Creamy Chicken-Vegetable Potpie

EGG-FREE, FAMILY-FRIENDLY, ONE-POT
SERVES 4 / PREP TIME: 10 MINUTES / COOK TIME: 20 MINUTES

I love potpie and how filling it is. But classic chicken potpie takes hours, so this quick version swaps in croutons for pie dough and uses a precooked rotisserie chicken so you'll be ready to get dinner on the table in just 30 minutes. Shorter time but still full of hearty flavor.

6 tablespoons olive oil (3 tablespoons used first, then 3 tablespoons used later)

1 small onion, chopped

2 celery stalks, halved lengthwise and cut into ¼-inch pieces

1 large carrot, quartered lengthwise and cut into ¼-inch pieces

1 cup frozen peas

½ teaspoon salt

¼ teaspoon pepper

2 tablespoons all-purpose flour

¾ cup water

¾ cup homemade Heavy Cream (see tip) or store-bought dairy-free heavy cream

1 store-bought rotisserie chicken, meat torn into ½-inch pieces

2 tablespoons finely chopped parsley

4 cups cubed crusty bread

½ cup dairy-free shredded Cheddar cheese

1. Preheat the oven to 400°F.

2. In a large skillet, heat 3 tablespoons of oil over medium heat. Add the onion, celery, carrot, peas, salt, and pepper; cook until crisp-tender, about 5 minutes.

3. Stir in the flour and cook for 1 minute. Increase the heat to medium-high and stir in the water and heavy cream; simmer, stirring occasionally, until slightly thickened, about 3 minutes. Stir in the chicken and parsley.

4. Transfer the chicken mixture to a shallow, 8-by-11-inch casserole dish. In a large bowl, toss together the bread cubes and the remaining 3 tablespoons of oil to coat. Scatter over the chicken mixture to cover and sprinkle with the cheese. Bake until the top is nicely toasted and the cheese is melted, about 15 minutes.

---

Ingredient Tip: Load up on as many veggies as you want. Go ahead and stir in chopped broccoli, cauliflower florets, or sliced cooked mushrooms for more flavor and to make it your own.

# Buffalo Chicken Fingers with Sour Cream & Chive Dip

**FAMILY-FRIENDLY**

SERVES 4 / PREP TIME: 10 MINUTES / COOK TIME: 18 MINUTES

This recipe takes Buffalo wing flavor and bakes it right into juicy, tender, spicy chicken strips. The sour cream–based dip keeps your palate cool. You can control the heat in this recipe by using more or less of the hot sauce.

2½ cups bread crumbs

1½ teaspoons salt

½ teaspoon pepper

4 large eggs or egg substitute (see tip)

4 chicken tenders

¼ cup olive oil

2 tablespoons homemade Butter or store-bought dairy-free butter, melted

6 tablespoons store-bought hot sauce

1½ cups homemade Sour Cream & Chive Dressing or store-bought dairy-free sour cream and chive dressing, for dipping

1. Preheat the oven to 425°F.
2. In a medium bowl, combine the bread crumbs, salt, and pepper. In a shallow bowl, beat the eggs.
3. Coat a chicken piece with the bread crumbs, dip in the eggs, then coat again with the bread crumbs; place on a plate. Repeat with the remaining chicken.

4. In a large skillet, heat the oil over medium-high heat until shimmering. Add half of the chicken tenders and cook, turning once, until golden, about 4 minutes. Transfer to a baking sheet. Repeat with the remaining chicken.

5. Bake chicken tenders in the preheated oven until cooked through, about 10 minutes.

6. In a small bowl, stir together the melted butter and hot sauce. Drizzle over the chicken and serve with the sour cream and chive dressing dipping sauce.

---

Substitution Tip: Cooking for kids? Leave out the hot sauce/butter sauce and swap in either a store-bought dairy-free Buffalo sauce or your favorite barbecue sauce.

# Sour Cream Mashed Potato–Stuffed Chicken

**EGG-FREE, FAMILY-FRIENDLY**
SERVES 4 / PREP TIME: 6 MINUTES / COOK TIME: 24 MINUTES

I love this take on stuffed chicken. Chicken thighs bake very well, staying juicy and tender in the oven and making this meal melt in your mouth. Chicken thighs can vary greatly in size, which means you may end up buying more than four. Just evenly divide the mashed potato filling so everyone has an equal serving, no matter the individual size.

**2 potatoes, peeled and cut into ½-inch chunks**

**¼ cup homemade Cashew Milk or store-bought dairy-free cashew milk**

**2 tablespoons homemade Sour Cream or store-bought dairy-free sour cream**

**2 tablespoons homemade Butter or store-bought dairy-free butter**

**Salt**

**Freshly ground black pepper**

**4 large bone-in, skin-on chicken thighs (about 2 pounds)**

**Olive oil, for drizzling**

**Chopped flat-leaf parsley, for topping**

1. Preheat the oven to 450°F.
2. In a medium saucepan, bring the potatoes and enough cold water to cover them completely to a boil; reduce the heat to medium and simmer until fork-tender, about 6 minutes. Drain and return the potatoes to the pot.

3. Add the milk, sour cream, and butter to the potatoes; mash until smooth and season with salt and pepper.

4. Run your fingers under the skin of each chicken thigh to separate it from the meat and stuff the area between the skin and meat with a quarter of the mashed potatoes, pressing gently to evenly distribute.

5. Place the stuffed chicken in a roasting pan. Drizzle with oil and season generously with salt and pepper; top with parsley. Roast in the oven, skin-side up, until cooked through, about 18 minutes.

---

Substitution Tip: The sour cream adds a nice tang to the mashed potatoes, but if you're a mashed potato purist, go ahead and swap in another 2 tablespoons of butter instead.

# Marsala Chicken Pasta Bake

**EGG-FREE, FAMILY-FRIENDLY, GOOD FOR LEFTOVERS**
SERVES 4 / PREP TIME: 10 MINUTES / COOK TIME: 20 MINUTES

This hearty pasta is perfect weeknight dinner material. If you already have chicken at home, go ahead and use it. Coarsely chop it and cook over medium-high heat until cooked through and season with salt and pepper. If you're not in the mood for pasta, this baked chicken marsala goes well with rice or herbed roasted potatoes. Store the leftovers in an airtight container in the refrigerator for up to 3 days.

½ pound penne pasta

2 tablespoons olive oil

1 (10-ounce) container sliced mushrooms

3 tablespoons all-purpose flour

1 cup marsala wine or dry white wine

1 cup store-bought chicken broth or water

½ cup homemade Heavy Cream (see tip) or store-bought dairy-free heavy cream (see chart)

2 packed cups coarsely chopped rotisserie chicken

2 tablespoons chopped parsley

Salt

Freshly ground black pepper

2 tablespoons homemade Grated Parmesan or store-bought dairy-free grated Parmesan

1. Preheat the oven to 425°F.

2. Cook the pasta in a large pot of boiling salted water until al dente, about 12 minutes; drain.

3. In a large skillet, heat the oil over medium-high heat and add the mushrooms; cook, stirring occasionally, until softened. Sprinkle over the flour and stir for 1 minute.

4. Stir in the marsala, broth, and heavy cream; simmer, stirring occasionally, until slightly thickened, about 3 minutes. Stir in the pasta, chicken, and parsley; season with salt and pepper.

5. Transfer the chicken mixture to a greased 11-by-7-inch casserole pan, spreading in an even layer. Top with the Parmesan and cover with foil; bake until bubbly, about 15 minutes.

---

Time-saving Tip: If you want to save even more time, just toss the chicken with the mushroom marsala sauce and sprinkle on some Parmesan instead of baking the pasta casserole-style.

# Turkey Sloppy Joe Pizza Pockets

**EGG-FREE, FAMILY-FRIENDLY, MAKE-AHEAD**
**SERVES 4 / PREP TIME: 10 MINUTES / COOK TIME: 20 MINUTES**

This fun mash-up recipe combines two classics—sloppy joe and pizza pockets—without the memorable mess. The store-bought pizza dough makes this recipe a quick one, and I hope you enjoy customizing your pizza pocket toppings. The Worcestershire sauce gives an incredible savory umami flavor both adults and kids will love. These easy pockets are great for freezing and pulling out for a quick meal. Just reheat in a 400°F oven until hot.

**2 tablespoons olive oil, plus more for greasing**

**1½ pounds ground turkey**

**1 red bell pepper, coarsely chopped**

**½ onion, coarsely chopped**

**1 cup store-bought dairy-free canned pizza sauce**

**1 tablespoon Worcestershire sauce**

**Salt**

**Freshly ground black pepper**

**1 pound store-bought pizza dough, at room temperature**

**2 cups store-bought dairy-free shredded mozzarella-style cheese**

1. Preheat the oven to 400°F. Lightly grease a baking sheet with oil.

2. In a large skillet, heat the oil over medium heat. Add the ground

turkey, bell pepper, and onion; cook over medium-high heat until the turkey is cooked through and the vegetables are tender, breaking up the meat into crumbles, about 6 minutes. Stir in the pizza sauce and Worcestershire sauce; season to taste with salt and pepper and let cool completely.

3. Divide the pizza dough into quarters and, working with 1 piece at a time, roll out into an 8-inch round. Place the rounds on the prepared baking sheet with about ⅓ of each round hanging over the baking sheet edges.

4. Place about 1 cup of the turkey mixture onto each round, leaving a ½-inch border on all sides. Top each with a quarter of the cheese and fold the dough over the filling; crimp the edges together to seal. Cut a small vent in the top of each pocket and bake until puffed and golden, about 14 minutes.

Substitution Tip: Swap in ground beef for the turkey. After cooking, just drain off any excess rendered fat if needed.

# Bacon-Wrapped Maple-Mustard Pork Tenderloin

EGG-FREE, FAMILY-FRIENDLY, NUT-FREE
SERVES 4 / PREP TIME: 10 MINUTES / COOK TIME: 15 MINUTES

This is a staple main dish for my family—bacon or not—because it cooks up in just 15 minutes. The maple syrup adds a bit of sweetness to the pork and the garlic herb mixture, and the mustard adds depth to the pork flavors.

- 2 tablespoons olive oil plus some for drizzling
- ¼ cup Dijon mustard
- 2 tablespoons maple syrup
- 2 teaspoons chopped fresh rosemary
- 2 teaspoons chopped fresh thyme
- 2 garlic cloves, finely chopped
- 2 (1-pound) pork tenderloins, patted dry
- 14 slices bacon

1. Preheat the oven to 425°F and line a baking sheet with parchment paper.
2. In a resealable plastic bag, mix together the olive oil, mustard, maple syrup, rosemary, thyme, and garlic. Add the pork and turn in the mixture to coat.
3. Arrange 7 bacon slices in a row onto a piece of plastic wrap. Overlap the bacon slightly, forming a rectangle the length of the tenderloin. Place 1 pork tenderloin on the bottom edge of the

bacon, then pick up the bottom edge of the plastic wrap and roll the bacon around the tenderloin; carefully remove the plastic wrap and place on the prepared baking sheet. Repeat with the remaining tenderloin and bacon; drizzle with olive oil and season with salt and pepper.

4. Roast the pork until a thermometer inserted into the center of the pork registers 145°F or the center is very light pink and juicy, about 15 minutes. Let rest for 5 minutes before slicing.

---

Ingredient Tip: For extra flavor, refrigerate the pork with the marinade for 1 hour or overnight to really soak in those flavors and make the pork more tender.

# Salsa Steak Tacos

EGG-FREE, FAMILY-FRIENDLY, GLUTEN-FREE, NUT-FREE
SERVES 4 / PREP TIME: 10 MINUTES / COOK TIME: 15 MINUTES

I love to make this low-maintenance taco dinner when I have impromptu outdoor get-togethers. The cola not only adds sweetness to the marinade but also helps the meat caramelize while it's cooking on the grill. An interesting fact: One lime has approximately 2 tablespoons of lime juice and about 2 teaspoons of zest.

FOR THE SALSA

**2 tomatoes, finely chopped**

**1 small onion, chopped**

**¼ cup finely chopped cilantro or parsley**

**2 jalapeño peppers, seeded and finely chopped**

**Juice of 1 lime, about 2 tablespoons**

**Salt**

FOR THE STEAK

**½ cup cola soda**

**2 tablespoons olive oil**

**Juice of 1 lime, about 2 tablespoons, plus lime wedges for serving**

**2 teaspoons chili powder**

**1½ teaspoons salt**

**1 pound skirt steak, cut into 4 portions**

**8 crisp corn taco shells**

**2 cups shredded coleslaw mix**

**1 avocado, cut into 8 slices lengthwise**

TO MAKE THE SALSA

In a large bowl, toss together the tomatoes, onion, cilantro, jalapeños, and lime juice; season with salt.

TO MAKE THE STEAK

1. In a resealable plastic bag, combine the cola, oil, lime juice, chili powder, and salt. Add the steak and turn in the mixture to coat completely.

2. Preheat a grill or grill pan to high. Grill the steak, turning once, about 15 minutes for medium-rare, either showing 135°F on a meat thermometer or having a warm dark pink center; let rest for 5 minutes.

3. Thinly slice the steak against the grain and toss with the tomato salsa. Fill each taco shell with the steak and salsa and top with some coleslaw mix and an avocado slice. Serve with the lime wedges.

Time-saving Tip: Short on time? Swap in store-bought salsa for the homemade salsa in the recipe, and you can also substitute 2 tablespoons of bottled lime juice for fresh lime juice in the steak marinade.

# Boursin-Style Cheese-Stuffed Burgers

**EGG-FREE, FAMILY-FRIENDLY**
SERVES 4 / PREP TIME: 8 MINUTES / COOK TIME: 7 MINUTES

This burger has an addictively creamy, cheesy center. For a juicy-on-the-inside and crispy-on-the-outside burger, salt the uncooked patties right before cooking. These burgers go well with sweet potato fries, which you can make by peeling and cutting raw sweet potatoes into strips and tossing the strips with oil, salt, pepper, and paprika. Place them in a single layer on a parchment-lined baking sheet and bake at 450°F for 15 to 20 minutes, turning occasionally.

**2 tablespoons homemade Cream Cheese or store-bought dairy-free cream cheese, at room temperature**

**1 garlic clove, finely chopped**

**1 tablespoon finely chopped parsley**

**2 teaspoons finely chopped chives**

**1 teaspoon Dijon mustard**

**Salt**

**1½ pounds ground beef**

**4 hamburger buns, split**

**Lettuce leaves, tomato slices, and sliced red onion, for serving**

1. In a small bowl, combine the cream cheese, garlic, parsley, chives, and mustard.

2. Shape the beef into 8 thin patties and season with salt. Spoon the cheese mixture onto the center of 4 patties and top with the

remaining patties, firmly pressing together the edges to seal.

3. Preheat a grill or grill pan over medium-high heat and oil the grate or pan; grill the burgers, turning once, about 7 minutes total for medium-rare. Serve the burgers on the buns with the toppings.

---

Substitution Tip: For a leaner option, you can use ground turkey or ground chicken in place of the ground beef and use Boston or iceberg lettuce instead of hamburger buns.

# Tex-Mex Meatloaf Pie

**FAMILY-FRIENDLY, NUT-FREE, ONE-POT**
SERVES 4 / PREP TIME: 5 MINUTES / COOK TIME: 25 MINUTES

This recipe turns standard meatloaf into a hearty and cheesy crustless pie. Change up the flavors by swapping in your favorite dairy-free jarred tomato sauce for the salsa.

- 1 (16-ounce) jar fire-roasted red peppers, drained, split, and seeded
- 3 cups store-bought shredded Cheddar cheese, divided
- 1½ pounds ground beef
- 1 (16-ounce) jar chunky salsa (¾ cup used first, the rest used later)
- 1 cup bread crumbs
- 2 large eggs or egg substitute (see tip), lightly beaten
- ¼ cup finely chopped cilantro or parsley
- ¾ teaspoon salt
- ¾ teaspoon pepper

1. Preheat the oven to 375°F.
2. Grease a 10-inch pie plate lightly with oil and line with the red peppers. Scatter 1 cup of cheese on top.
3. In a large bowl, mix the beef, 1 cup of cheese, ¾ cup of salsa, the bread crumbs, eggs, parsley, salt, and pepper until just combined.
4. Press the meat mixture into the pepper-lined pie plate. Spread the remaining salsa and cheese over the top and bake until cooked through, about 25 minutes; let cool for about 5 minutes before serving.

Substitution Tip: Use a store-bought prebaked pie shell instead of the layer of red peppers if you want a more traditional meat pie. Just press the pie shell into the pie plate, top with the meatloaf mixture, cheese, and salsa, and bake in the same way.

# Crispy Fish Sticks with Sweet Relish Tartar Sauce

**EGG-FREE, FAMILY-FRIENDLY, MAKE-AHEAD**
**SERVES 4 / PREP TIME: 12 MINUTES / COOK TIME: 12 MINUTES**

I love the crispy corn-flake coating, seasoned with just the right amount of paprika. It adds a delightful crunch to this family favorite. While you fry the remaining fish sticks in batches, keep the cooked ones warm in a preheated 250°F oven.

### FOR THE TARTAR SAUCE

1 cup homemade Egg-Free Mayonnaise or store-bought mayonnaise

2 tablespoons mustard

¼ cup sweet relish

1 tablespoon lemon juice

1 tablespoon finely chopped dill

Salt

Freshly ground black pepper

### FOR THE FISH STICKS

3 cups corn flakes

2 tablespoons paprika

1 tablespoon sugar

1 tablespoon salt

½ teaspoon pepper

¾ cup Egg-Free Mayonnaise or store-bought mayonnaise

¼ cup mustard

Neutral-tasting oil, for frying

2 pounds halibut or cod fillets, cut into ½-inch-wide strips

Salt

Freshly ground black pepper

### TO MAKE THE TARTAR SAUCE

In a small bowl, stir together the mayonnaise, mustard, relish, lemon juice, and dill; season with salt and pepper and refrigerate.

### TO MAKE THE FISH STICKS

1. In a food processor, combine the corn flakes, paprika, sugar, salt, and pepper. Pulse until coarsely chopped and transfer to a shallow bowl.

2. In a separate shallow bowl, combine the mayonnaise and mustard.

3. Heat about 1 inch of oil in a deep, heavy-bottomed skillet over medium heat until it measures 350°F on a deep-fry thermometer.

4. Season the fish with salt and pepper. Working in batches, dredge the fish strips in the mayonnaise and mustard mixture, then coat completely with the corn flake mixture. Add to the hot oil and fry, turning once, until golden and cooked through, about 3 minutes total. Remove with a slotted spoon and drain on paper towels; season with salt. Repeat with the remaining fish. Serve with the tartar sauce.

Time-saving Tip: You can make a double batch of these and store the leftover uncooked fish sticks in a single layer in a resealable bag for up to 1 month in the freezer.

# Fried Shrimp with Creamy Coleslaw

CALCIUM-RICH, FAMILY-FRIENDLY

SERVES 4 / PREP TIME: 15 MINUTES / COOK TIME: 6 MINUTES

For this shrimp, I wanted a light, tempura-like coating, which is why I use cornstarch. If you feel like splurging, go ahead and use jumbo shrimp. Just add a minute or so to the cooking time.

### FOR THE COLESLAW

**2 cups coleslaw mix**

**½ cup homemade Egg-Free Mayonnaise or store-bought mayonnaise**

**1½ teaspoons apple cider vinegar**

**1 teaspoon honey**

**¼ teaspoon celery seeds**

**Salt**

**Freshly ground black pepper**

### FOR THE FRIED SHRIMP

**Vegetable oil, for frying**

**¾ cup all-purpose flour**

**¾ cup cornstarch**

**1 teaspoon salt**

**½ teaspoon pepper**

**2 large eggs or egg substitute (see tip)**

**1 pound medium shrimp, peeled and deveined**

**TO MAKE THE COLESLAW**

In a medium bowl, toss together the coleslaw mix, mayonnaise, vinegar, honey, and celery seeds; season with salt and pepper and refrigerate until ready to serve.

**TO MAKE THE FRIED SHRIMP**

1. Heat about 2 inches oil in a deep, heavy-bottomed skillet over medium heat until it measures 350°F on a deep-fry thermometer.

2. In a shallow bowl, whisk together the flour, cornstarch, salt, and pepper. In another shallow bowl, beat together the eggs.

3. Working in batches, dredge the shrimp in the flour mixture, shake off any excess, dip in the beaten eggs, then dredge again in the flour mixture; add to the hot oil and fry until golden, turning once, about 2 minutes. Using a slotted spoon, transfer to paper towels to drain. Repeat with the remaining shrimp, returning the oil to 350°F between batches.

4. Serve with the creamy coleslaw.

Cooking Tip: If you don't have a deep-fry thermometer or want a baked version of these yummy shrimp, preheat the oven to 475°F and place a wire rack on a baking sheet; spray with dairy-free cooking spray. Place the coated shrimp on the rack and spray the shrimp with cooking spray; bake, turning once, until cooked through and crisp, about 6 minutes.

# Spicy Chipotle Shrimp

EGG-FREE, GLUTEN-FREE, NUT-FREE
SERVES 4 / PREP TIME: 6 MINUTES / COOK TIME: 9 MINUTES

Dinner can't get any easier than this 15-minute shrimp dish. I like to spoon the shrimp over rice or in a warm tortilla with all the fixings for a great taco. You can easily dial down the spice level to make this more kid friendly.

1 (15-ounce) can fire-roasted crushed tomatoes

2 tablespoons olive oil

2 chipotle chiles in adobo sauce

3 garlic cloves

½ cup water

1 teaspoon salt

1 pound medium shrimp, peeled and deveined

Cilantro or parsley, chopped, for topping

1. In a blender or food processor, combine the tomatoes, oil, chipotle chiles, garlic, and water until smooth; season with salt.

2. Transfer to a large skillet and cook until heated through, about 5 minutes.

3. Add the shrimp and cook, stirring occasionally, until cooked through, about 4 minutes; top with the cilantro for serving.

Substitution Tip: Can't find fire-roasted crushed tomatoes at your supermarket? Just use regular crushed tomatoes to get the same consistency but a less smoky flavor.

# Poached Salmon with Dill Pickle Mayo

**CALCIUM-RICH, EGG-FREE, GLUTEN-FREE, GOOD FOR LEFTOVERS**
**SERVES 4 / PREP TIME: 10 MINUTES / COOK TIME: 10 MINUTES**

I love the cooking method of poaching salmon in a foil pack because it creates less mess and doesn't make the whole house smell like fish. The dill pickle mayo complements the salmon perfectly. If you're lucky, you'll have some left over to use as a condiment on a burger or sandwich.

**4 (1-inch thick) salmon fillets (about 1½ pounds)**

**Olive oil, for drizzling**

**Salt**

**Freshly ground black pepper**

**½ cup homemade <u>Egg-Free Mayonnaise</u> or store-bought mayonnaise**

**Juice and zest of ½ lemon**

**1 large dill pickle, finely chopped**

**1 teaspoon finely chopped scallions**

1. Bring a large pot of water to a boil.
2. Cut four 10-by-18-inch sheets of heavy-duty aluminum foil. Place each salmon fillet on one sheet of foil and drizzle with oil; season with salt and pepper. Fold the foil over the salmon to enclose; pressing out any air. Fold the foil on the sides to seal. Carefully drop the packets into the boiling water, cover, and cook until just firm to the touch, about 10 minutes.

3. In a small bowl, combine the mayonnaise, lemon juice and zest, pickle, and scallions; season with salt and pepper.

4. Transfer each foil packet to a plate and carefully cut open. Dollop the salmon with the dill pickle mayo.

---

Cooking Tip: If you are not comfortable with poaching the salmon, you can choose to cook it however you prefer. For grilling, place the fillets skin-side down on a foil-covered baking sheet and grill over medium heat for 15 to 20 minutes. For baking, place the salmon fillets skin-side down on a foil-covered baking sheet and bake at 400°F for 15 minutes. If you prefer cooking them on the stovetop, place the salmon skin-side up in an oiled pan over medium-high heat and cook for about 4 minutes, turn over, and cook for an additional 3 minutes until the salmon is firm to the touch and skin is crisp.

**Dulce de Leche–Stuffed Gingerbread Whoopie Pies**

# CHAPTER EIGHT

# Desserts

Chocolate Brownie Crinkle Cookies

PB&J Cookies

S'mores Cookie Sandwiches

Dulce de Leche–Stuffed Gingerbread Whoopie Pies

Chocolate-Coconut Magic Bars

Chocolate Pudding with Whipped Cream

Toasted Coconut Snowball Cupcakes

Golden Birthday Cupcakes with Chocolate Frosting

Ice Cream Sundae Bonbons

Mini Strawberry Shortcakes

Powdered Cake Doughnuts

Fried Cinnamon-Sugar Fritters

# Chocolate Brownie Crinkle Cookies

FAMILY-FRIENDLY, NUT-FREE, VEGETARIAN
MAKES 32 / PREP TIME: 16 MINUTES / COOK TIME: 14 MINUTES

These cookies have a surprising brownie texture and flavor with an irresistible crunchy exterior. Sometimes I like to sandwich these cookies with a dairy-free chocolate hazelnut spread or dairy-free ice cream to make fun cookie sandwiches.

2½ cups dairy-free chocolate chips (2 cups used first, ½ cup used later)

2 tablespoons nonhydrogenated shortening or homemade Butter or store-bought dairy-free butter, at room temperature

¼ cup plus 2 tablespoons all-purpose flour (used all at once)

1 teaspoon baking powder

¼ teaspoon salt

2 large eggs or egg substitute (see tip), at room temperature

½ cup granulated sugar

1 teaspoon pure vanilla extract

1. Preheat the oven to 350°F. Line 2 baking sheets with parchment paper.
2. In a medium, microwavable bowl, melt together 2 cups of chocolate chips and the shortening on medium power in the microwave until almost melted, about 1½ minutes; stir just until smooth.
3. In a small bowl, whisk together the flour, baking powder, and

salt. Using a stand mixer fitted with the whip attachment, beat together the eggs, sugar, and vanilla at high speed until thickened and fluffy, about 5 minutes.

4. Mix in the melted chocolate at medium speed, then whisk in the flour mixture. Stir in the remaining ½ cup of chocolate chips. Refrigerate the dough until firm enough to scoop but still soft, about 10 minutes.

5. Drop rounded tablespoons of dough 2 inches apart on the prepared baking sheets; bake, switching and rotating the pans halfway through baking, until the cookies appear bubbly but are soft, about 14 minutes. Let cool for about 2 minutes, then, using a spatula, transfer to a wire rack to cool completely.

Cooking Tips: If you want the signature crinkle look, roll the cookie dough balls in confectioners' sugar to coat completely before baking. If you don't have a stand mixer with a whip attachment, you can use a regular hand mixer.

# PB&J Cookies

**FAMILY-FRIENDLY, VEGETARIAN**
MAKES 20 / PREP TIME: 16 MINUTES / COOK TIME: 14 MINUTES

Peanut butter and jelly aren't just for school lunches anymore. Now, you can eat this quintessential flavor combination in a cookie any time. I love to include the kids and let them draw patterns on the cookies with the peanut butter frosting. You can also add 1 or 2 drops of food coloring to the frosting to make decorating even more fun.

**FOR THE COOKIES**

½ cup all-purpose flour

½ teaspoon baking powder

¾ cup creamy peanut butter

¼ cup nonhydrogenated shortening or homemade Butter or store-bought dairy-free butter, at room temperature

¾ cup granulated sugar

¼ cup brown sugar

1 large egg or egg substitute (see tip)

3 tablespoons plus 1 teaspoon strawberry jelly (used all at once)

**FOR THE FROSTING**

¼ cup creamy peanut butter

¼ cup plus 2 tablespoons confectioners' sugar (used all at once)

1½ tablespoons homemade Cashew Milk or store-bought dairy-free cashew milk

### TO MAKE THE COOKIES

1. Preheat the oven to 350°F.

2. In a small bowl, stir together the flour and baking powder.

3. Using a large bowl and mixer, blend the peanut butter with the shortening on medium speed. Add the granulated sugar and brown sugar and beat until smooth. Beat in the egg until incorporated. Stir in the flour mixture until just combined.

4. Using a 1½-inch ice cream scoop or a tablespoon, drop the dough 2 inches apart on 2 ungreased baking sheets. Using your thumb, gently dent the center of each cookie. Spoon about ½ teaspoon of jelly into each center. Bake until lightly golden, about 12 minutes. Transfer to a wire rack to cool completely.

### TO MAKE THE FROSTING

In a small bowl, beat together the peanut butter and the confectioners' sugar. Whisk in the milk, a little at a time, until the frosting reaches a good consistency for piping. Using a resealable sandwich bag with a tiny corner snipped off, pipe the frosting over the cookies in a zigzag pattern.

---

**Time-saving Tip:** Short on time? Leave the peanut butter frosting off and still get that PB&J flavor combination in the cookie itself. You can also use a stand mixer for these cookies instead of a hand mixer.

# S'mores Cookie Sandwiches

**FAMILY-FRIENDLY, NUT-FREE**
SERVES 4 / PREP TIME: 10 MINUTES / COOK TIME: 12 MINUTES

If you can't get to a campfire anytime soon, you can still enjoy s'mores at home. These cookies are bursting with chocolate chips and crushed graham crackers, then sandwiched with marshmallow.

½ cup nonhydrogenated shortening or homemade Butter or store-bought dairy-free butter, at room temperature

¾ cup packed dark brown sugar

1 large egg or egg substitute (see tip)

½ teaspoon salt

½ teaspoon baking powder

½ teaspoon baking soda

1 teaspoon pure vanilla extract

1 cup plus 2 tablespoons all-purpose flour (used all at once)

1 cup dairy-free chocolate chips

½ cup coarsely crushed graham crackers

10 tablespoons marshmallow cream

1. Preheat the oven to 350°F. Line 2 baking sheets with parchment paper.

2. Using a mixer, cream the shortening and brown sugar until fluffy, about 5 minutes. Beat in the egg.

3. Mix in the salt, baking powder, and baking soda at low speed, then mix in the vanilla and flour. Stir in the chocolate chips and crushed graham crackers.

4. Place 10 rounded tablespoonfuls of dough onto the prepared baking sheets; bake until golden at the edges and slightly soft in the center, about 12 minutes. Transfer to a wire rack to cool completely.

5. Sandwich the cookies with 2 tablespoons marshmallow cream each.

Ingredient Tip: If you want to get even more graham cracker flavor, process 4 graham crackers in a blender or food processor until finely crushed to yield ¼ cup, then swap them in for ¼ cup of the flour.

# Dulce de Leche–Stuffed Gingerbread Whoopie Pies

FAMILY-FRIENDLY, VEGETARIAN
MAKES 10 WHOOPIE PIES / PREP TIME: 15 MINUTES / COOK TIME: 10 MINUTES

This recipe will keep you cozy—and happy—through the autumn and winter seasons. The dulce de leche complements the sweet molasses and draws out the comforting spices in the gingerbread cake cookies.

1½ cups all-purpose flour

2 tablespoons unsweetened cocoa powder

2 teaspoons ground ginger

1 teaspoon pumpkin pie spice

1½ teaspoons baking powder

½ teaspoon baking soda

½ teaspoon salt

½ cup neutral-flavored oil

½ cup packed light brown sugar

3 tablespoons unsulfured molasses

1 large egg or egg substitute (see tip), at room temperature, lightly beaten

½ cup homemade Dulce de Leche or store-bought dairy-free dulce de leche

Confectioners' sugar, for dusting

1. Preheat the oven to 350°F and line two baking sheets with parchment paper.
2. In a medium bowl, whisk together the flour, cocoa powder,

ginger, pumpkin pie spice, baking powder, baking soda, and salt.

3. In a large bowl, whisk together the oil and brown sugar until smooth, then whisk in the molasses and egg. Fold in the flour mixture until just combined.

4. Using a 1½-inch ice cream scoop or a rounded tablespoon, drop mounds of batter, evenly spaced, onto the prepared baking sheets. Bake until springy to the touch, about 10 minutes. Transfer to a wire rack to cool completely.

5. To assemble, spread the flat side of 10 cookies with about 2 teaspoons dulce de leche and top with the remaining cookies. Dust with confectioners' sugar.

# Chocolate-Coconut Magic Bars

**EGG-FREE, FAMILY-FRIENDLY, VEGETARIAN**
MAKES 16 BARS / PREP TIME: 5 MINUTES / COOK TIME: 25 MINUTES

This recipe reminds me of my childhood. I had been dreaming of these impossibly rich bars, layered with graham crackers, chocolate chips, and coconut for years until I figured out how to make Condensed Milk.

1 cup finely ground graham cracker crumbs

½ cup quick-cooking oats

⅛ teaspoon salt

⅓ cup nonhydrogenated shortening or homemade Butter or store-bought dairy-free butter, melted

1 cup dairy-free chocolate chips

1 cup sweetened flaked coconut

1 cup homemade Condensed Milk or store-bought dairy-free condensed milk

1. Preheat the oven to 350°F and line an 8-inch square baking pan with a 12-inch-long sheet of parchment paper.

2. In a small bowl, combine the graham cracker crumbs, oats, salt, and melted shortening; press into the pan. Scatter the chocolate chips and coconut over the mixture. Pour the condensed milk evenly over the top.

3. Bake until golden, about 25 minutes. Transfer to a wire rack to cool slightly; cut into 16 squares.

Time-saving Tip: Short on time? You can now pick up a can of dairy-free condensed milk in most natural food stores ([Resources](Resources)).

# Chocolate Pudding with Whipped Cream

**GLUTEN-FREE, FAMILY-FRIENDLY, VEGETARIAN**
SERVES 4 / PREP TIME: 10 MINUTES / COOK TIME: 10 MINUTES

This may well be everyone's favorite dessert—and for good reason. If you want to bring this pudding to the next level visually, layer the pudding and whipped cream twice for a stunning presentation similar to a parfait and top with a cherry or your favorite chopped nuts.

**8 ounces dairy-free chocolate, chopped**

**2 to 3 tablespoons unsweetened cocoa powder, sifted**

**3 cups store-bought dairy-free half-and-half**

**½ cup sugar**

**1 large egg plus 2 egg yolks or egg substitute (see tip)**

**1 cup homemade Whipped Cream or store-bought dairy-free whipped cream**

1. In a medium bowl, mix the chocolate and cocoa powder.

2. In a medium, heavy saucepan, heat the half-and-half over medium-high heat until it is almost boiling and bubbles form around the edges.

3. In a heatproof bowl, whisk together the sugar and eggs until thick and pale yellow, about 2 minutes. Slowly add half of the hot half-and-half to the egg mixture while whisking vigorously and then pour the mixture into the saucepan with the rest of the half-and-half; bring just to a boil over medium heat and cook, whisking constantly, until bubbly and thickened, 1 minute.

4. Pour the custard through a sieve into the reserved chocolate-cocoa mixture and whisk until smooth. Transfer the pudding to a rimmed baking sheet, spreading evenly; let cool slightly, then press plastic wrap onto the surface to cover and refrigerate until cold, about 20 minutes. To serve, top with the whipped cream.

---

Cooking Tip: This method of adding half of the hot liquid to the eggs before adding it all back into the hot saucepan to make custard is called "tempering eggs." You temper the eggs to slowly bring up the egg mixture to a higher temperature. If you just added all of it together without tempering, you would end up with cooked scrambled eggs instead of a smooth custard.

# Toasted Coconut Snowball Cupcakes

**FAMILY-FRIENDLY**
MAKES 12 / PREP TIME: 5 MINUTES / COOK TIME: 25 MINUTES

These may not completely resemble the convenience-store staple I grew up with as an occasional after-school treat, but they do come incredibly close in flavor.

**FOR THE CUPCAKES**

2 cups all-purpose flour

2 teaspoons baking powder

1 teaspoon ground cinnamon

½ teaspoon ground nutmeg

¼ teaspoon salt

¾ cup granulated sugar

1 cup sweetened flaked coconut, toasted and cooled

1 (13.5-ounce) can unsweetened coconut milk

½ cup nonhydrogenated shortening or homemade Butter or store-bought dairy-free butter, melted

2 large eggs or egg substitute (see tip), lightly beaten

2 teaspoons pure vanilla extract

**FOR THE FROSTING**

1 cup nonhydrogenated shortening or homemade Butter or store-bought dairy-free butter, at room temperature

½ cup confectioners' sugar

**1 (7.5-ounce) jar marshmallow cream**

**2 cups sweetened flaked coconut, toasted and cooled**

## TO MAKE THE CUPCAKES

1. Preheat the oven to 375°F and grease and flour a 12-cup muffin pan.

2. In a large bowl, sift the flour, baking powder, cinnamon, nutmeg, and salt together. Stir in the granulated sugar and toasted coconut.

3. In a small bowl, stir together the coconut milk, melted shortening, eggs, and vanilla. Add to the dry ingredients and stir until just combined.

4. Transfer the batter into the prepared pan, filling each cup about three-quarters full and bake until lightly golden and a toothpick inserted comes out clean, about 25 minutes. Transfer to a wire rack to cool completely.

## TO MAKE THE FROSTING

1. In a large bowl, beat the room-temperature shortening until creamy. Beat in half the confectioners' sugar until fluffy, then beat in the remainder. Add the marshmallow cream and beat until combined. If the mixture is too thick to squeeze through a pastry bag, stir in water to thin, 1 tablespoon at a time.

2. Fill a pastry bag with about ⅔ cup of the marshmallow frosting. Insert the tip of the pastry bag into the top of each cupcake and squeeze frosting into the center. Spread the rest of the frosting on the top, sides, and bottom and sprinkle the cupcakes with toasted coconut to coat.

Cooking Tip: If you don't have a pastry bag, just snip the corner off a resealable plastic bag to squeeze the frosting into the cupcakes, cutting out some of the cupcake center with a small knife if necessary.

# Golden Birthday Cupcakes with Chocolate Frosting

FAMILY-FRIENDLY, MAKE-AHEAD, VEGETARIAN
MAKES 12 / PREP TIME: 10 MINUTES / COOK TIME: 20 MINUTES

These golden cupcakes get a double dose of vanilla to deliver extra flavor to the classic birthday cake combination of vanilla and chocolate. The longer the frosting sits at room temperature, the more spreadable it gets. The chocolate frosting can be made ahead of time and refrigerated in an airtight container for up to 3 days. Just return to room temperature before using. The frosted cupcakes can be stored in an airtight container for up to 2 days.

**FOR THE FROSTING**

**4 ounces dairy-free chocolate, finely chopped**

**½ cup homemade Heavy Cream (see tip) or store-bought dairy-free heavy cream (see chart)**

**3 tablespoons nonhydrogenated shortening, at room temperature**

**1 tablespoon light corn syrup**

**Salt**

**FOR THE CUPCAKES**

**1½ cups all-purpose flour**

**2 teaspoons baking powder**

**½ teaspoon salt**

**½ cup nonhydrogenated shortening, at room temperature**

**¾ cup granulated sugar**

**2 large eggs or egg substitute (see tip), at room temperature**

1 vanilla bean, split lengthwise, seeds scraped

2 teaspoons pure vanilla extract

½ cup homemade [Cashew Milk](#) or store-bought dairy-free cashew milk, at room temperature

Sprinkles, for topping

### TO MAKE THE FROSTING

Place the chocolate in a medium bowl. In a small saucepan, heat the heavy cream with 3 tablespoons of shortening, corn syrup, and a pinch of salt until hot but not boiling; pour over the chocolate and let stand for 5 minutes, then whisk until smooth. Let the frosting cool, whisking occasionally, until thick enough for glazing the cupcakes, about 20 minutes.

### TO MAKE THE CUPCAKES

1. Preheat the oven to 350°F and line a 12-cup muffin pan with paper liners.

2. In a medium bowl, whisk the flour with the baking powder and salt.

3. In another medium bowl, using a handheld electric mixer, beat the shortening and the granulated sugar at medium speed until fluffy, about 3 minutes. Beat in the eggs, one at a time, then beat in the vanilla bean seeds and vanilla extract.

4. With the mixer on low speed, beat in half the flour mixture, then the milk, followed by the remaining flour mixture, until combined.

5. Divide the batter among the muffin cups, filling each about two-thirds full; bake until a toothpick inserted comes out clean, about 20 minutes. Transfer to a wire rack to cool completely. Spread the top of the cupcakes with the frosting and top with sprinkles.

Substitution Tip: **If you don't have vanilla bean on hand, just swap in an extra teaspoon of pure vanilla extract.**

# Ice Cream Sundae Bonbons

5-INGREDIENT, FAMILY-FRIENDLY, MAKE-AHEAD, VEGETARIAN
MAKES 25 / PREP TIME: 5 MINUTES / COOK TIME: 20 MINUTES

If you can keep yourself from eating the ingredients while preparing this recipe, these bonbons are almost instant gratification. Depending on the temperature in your kitchen, your bonbons may get a little melty. Just freeze as needed.

**16 ounces (2 cups) dairy-free chocolate, chopped or chocolate chips**

**25 plain vanilla cookies**

**1 pint dairy-free ice cream, vanilla or your favorite flavor**

**25 small maraschino cherries, stems removed**

**Rainbow sprinkles, for topping**

1. In a double boiler, melt about three-quarters of the chocolate; remove from the heat and stir in the remaining chocolate until melted; let cool slightly.

2. Place the cookies flat-side down on a parchment paper–lined baking sheet. Working quickly, top each cookie with 1 small scoop of ice cream and a cherry; dunk each bonbon into the chocolate to coat and top with sprinkles; return to the prepared baking sheet and freeze until firm, about 20 minutes.

Cooking Tip: If you do not have a double boiler, make your own by using a heatproof bowl set over a saucepan of boiling water.

# Mini Strawberry Shortcakes

FAMILY-FRIENDLY, VEGETARIAN
MAKES 36 / PREP TIME: 15 MINUTES / COOK TIME: 12 MINUTES

These definitely score cuteness points. These shortcakes are a great single-bite dessert, especially at summer backyard barbecues and block parties. They are fresh and feel light, and the smaller size makes for an interesting spin on the original. Interesting food fact: Mixing fruit with sugar or liquid is called "macerating" fruit. It's similar to the way you marinate meat.

2½ cups all-purpose flour

¼ cup light brown sugar

2 teaspoons baking powder

½ teaspoon salt

¾ cup cold nonhydrogenated shortening, cut into small pieces

1 large egg or egg substitute (see tip)

1 cup homemade Heavy Cream (see tip) or store-bought dairy-free heavy cream (see chart)

3 cups strawberries, hulled and sliced

1 tablespoon fresh lemon juice

1 tablespoon granulated sugar

1 cup homemade Whipped Cream or store-bought dairy-free whipped cream

1. Preheat the oven to 400°F and line a baking sheet with parchment paper.

2. Using an electric mixer, beat the flour with the brown sugar, baking powder, and salt. Add the shortening and mix on low

until crumbly.

3. In a small bowl, whisk together the egg and heavy cream. Add the liquid to the dry ingredients and mix until just combined.

4. On a clean, dry surface, pat the dough out until about 1 inch thick, and, using a 1½-inch biscuit cutter, cookie cutter, or juice glass, cut out rounds and place about 1 inch apart on the prepared baking sheet; bake until lightly golden and a toothpick inserted in the center comes out clean, about 12 minutes. Transfer to a wire rack and let cool completely.

5. While the shortcakes are baking, place the strawberries in a medium bowl and sprinkle with the lemon juice and granulated sugar; gently toss.

6. To serve, cut each shortcake in half and top the bottom halves with strawberries, whipped cream, and the shortcake tops. If you have leftover whipped cream, add a dollop to the top of each of your shortcakes.

---

Cooking Tip: To keep your biscuit cutter from sticking to the dough as you make the rounds, dip it in a small bowl of flour before making each cut.

# Powdered Cake Doughnuts

FAMILY-FRIENDLY, VEGETARIAN
MAKES 10 / PREP TIME: 15 MINUTES / COOK TIME: 12 MINUTES

There's something about doughnuts that makes people happy—even when their faces are covered in confectioners' sugar. I prefer these fluffy baked doughnuts over the often-heavier fried version. Doughnuts may have originated in England, but they are a staple everywhere now, including in my kitchen. Store the doughnuts in a plastic bag to prevent drying out at room temperature for 2 to 3 days or in the refrigerator for up to 1 week.

**1½ cups all-purpose flour**

**1 cup sugar**

**2 teaspoons baking powder**

**¼ teaspoon nutmeg**

**½ teaspoon salt**

**2 large eggs or egg substitute (see tip), at room temperature**

**¼ cup neutral-tasting oil**

**½ cup homemade Cashew Milk or store-bought dairy-free cashew milk**

**Confectioners' sugar, sifted, for coating**

1. Preheat the oven to 350°F and spray two nonstick 6-cavity doughnut pans with cooking spray.

2. In a large bowl, whisk together the flour, sugar, baking powder, nutmeg, and salt.

3. In a medium bowl, whisk together the eggs, oil, and milk until combined; add to the flour mixture and whisk until combined.

4. Spoon the batter into 10 cavities of the prepared doughnut pans until about three-quarters full; bake until a toothpick inserted in the center of a doughnut comes out clean, about 18 minutes. Let the doughnuts cool slightly, then place some confectioners' sugar on a plate and dredge the doughnuts to coat completely.

---

Time-saving Tip: **You can make these doughnuts ahead of time and freeze the baked uncoated doughnuts for 2 to 3 months. To freeze, wrap the doughnuts tightly in foil or plastic wrap or put in a heavy-duty airtight freezer bag.**

# Fried Cinnamon-Sugar Fritters

FAMILY-FRIENDLY, VEGETARIAN
MAKES 24 / PREP TIME: 10 MINUTES / COOK TIME: 8 MINUTES

These fritters are wonderfully fluffy and light thanks to the ricotta. I love to roll the hot fritters in cinnamon sugar to give them some sweetness.

½ cup plus 2 tablespoons sugar (½ cup used first, then 2 tablespoons used later)

2 teaspoons ground cinnamon

½ teaspoon salt (¼ teaspoons used first, then ¼ teaspoon used later)

1 cup all-purpose flour

1 tablespoon baking powder

Finely grated zest of 1 lemon

2 large eggs or egg substitute (see tip), lightly beaten

1 cup homemade Ricotta or store-bought dairy-free ricotta

1 tablespoon pure vanilla extract

Neutral-flavored oil, for frying

1. In a medium shallow bowl, combine ½ cup of sugar, cinnamon, and ¼ teaspoon of salt.

2. In a large bowl, whisk the flour with the remaining 2 tablespoons of sugar, baking powder, lemon zest, and remaining ¼ teaspoon of salt. Add the eggs, ricotta, and vanilla and stir just to combine.

3. In a large saucepan, heat 2 inches of oil to 365°F. Line a baking rack with paper towels. Using a small ice cream scoop or

tablespoon, scoop rounded tablespoons of batter into the hot oil. Fry, turning once, until the fritters are golden and cooked through, about 4 minutes; drain on paper towels for 30 seconds, then transfer them to the cinnamon sugar and toss to coat. Repeat with the remaining batter working in batches. Serve the fritters hot.

Substitution Tip: If you are a chocolate lover, stir ⅓ cup dairy-free mini chocolate chips into the batter before frying.

**Classic Party Fondue**

# CHAPTER NINE

## Sauces & Dressings

Béchamel

Garlicky Dijon Steak Sauce

Cheese Sauce

Classic Party Fondue

Country Gravy

Egg-Free Mayonnaise

Creamy Poppy Seed Vinaigrette

Ranch Dressing

Caesar Parmesan Dressing

Sour Cream & Chive Dressing

# Béchamel

5-INGREDIENT, EGG-FREE, FAMILY-FRIENDLY, VEGAN
MAKES 1½ CUPS / PREP TIME: 2 MINUTES / COOK TIME: 10 MINUTES

I have been known to eat this classically milk-based French white cream sauce with a spoon. Béchamel gives any recipe body and richness. Depending on your needs, you can thin it and stir it into soups or use it as a base for macaroni and cheese.

**2 tablespoons olive oil or melted homemade Butter or store-bought dairy-free butter**

**2 tablespoons all-purpose flour**

**1½ cups homemade Cashew Milk or store-bought dairy-free cashew milk**

**1 teaspoon salt**

**¼ teaspoon ground nutmeg**

In a small saucepan, heat the oil over medium heat. Whisk in the flour and stir until smooth. Slowly whisk in the milk and cook, stirring, until thickened, about 10 minutes. Season with the salt and nutmeg.

Substitution Tip: If you love garlic and want to flavor this creamy sauce more, cook 2 finely chopped garlic cloves in the olive oil until golden before adding the flour and milk.

# Garlicky Dijon Steak Sauce

EGG-FREE, FAMILY-FRIENDLY, MAKE-AHEAD, VEGAN
MAKES 1 CUP / PREP TIME: 5 MINUTES

Don't limit this sauce to steak. It's great as a burger topping or slathered on a roast beef sandwich. The steak sauce can be kept refrigerated in a resealable container for up to 1 week. An interesting fact about horseradish is that it is included in the Brassicaceae family and is closely related to wasabi, mustard, broccoli, and cabbage. Horseradish is nutrient-rich and has a lot of fiber, vitamin C, potassium, calcium, magnesium, and zinc. This root is great for a little spicy kick of flavor.

**¼ cup olive oil**

**3 tablespoons store-bought prepared horseradish**

**3 tablespoons Dijon mustard**

**2 tablespoons whole-grain mustard**

**1 shallot, finely chopped**

**1 tablespoon chives, coarsely chopped**

**Pinch cayenne pepper**

**2 to 4 tablespoons water**

**Salt**

**Freshly ground black pepper**

In a small bowl, whisk together the oil, horseradish sauce, Dijon mustard, whole-grain mustard, shallot, chives, and cayenne. Whisk in water, 1 tablespoon at a time, until you reach your preferred consistency and season with salt and pepper.

Substitution Tip: **Have fresh herbs in the garden? Swap in tarragon or parsley for the chives in this recipe.**

# Cheese Sauce

EGG-FREE, FAMILY-FRIENDLY, GLUTEN-FREE, MAKE-AHEAD, VEGAN
MAKES 2 CUPS / PREP TIME: 18 MINUTES

This versatile sauce is made with neutral-flavored cashews and nutritional yeast, a deactivated yeast with a salty, cheesy flavor. The red bell pepper lends flavor and gives the sauce its Cheddar-like color. This sauce is great over meat, vegetables, and potatoes and is featured in my Stovetop Mac & Cheese recipe. This cheese sauce can be kept refrigerated in a resealable container for up to 1 week.

**2 cups raw cashews, soaked in hot water for 15 minutes, then rinsed and drained**

**½ cup red bell pepper, seeded and chopped**

**1 garlic clove, finely chopped**

**½ cup neutral-flavored oil**

**1 tablespoon lemon juice**

**2 tablespoons nutritional yeast**

**2 teaspoons salt**

**½ cup water**

Blend together the cashews, bell pepper, garlic, oil, lemon juice, nutritional yeast, salt, and water in a high-speed blender or food processor, scraping down the sides, until smooth. Add more water, if necessary, 1 tablespoon at a time, until creamy.

Ingredient Tip: Heat things up by adding a seeded, chopped jalapeño pepper to the blender before processing.

# Classic Party Fondue

EGG-FREE, FAMILY-FRIENDLY, VEGAN
MAKES 2 CUPS / PREP TIME: 5 MINUTES / COOK TIME: 10 MINUTES

This knockoff cheesy dipping sauce is pure indulgence. The miso paste adds a surprising fermented, cheese-like depth of flavor while the xanthan gum gives the sauce that classic stretch. Fondue is a party classic and is great for sharing. Serve the fondue with bread cubes, apple slices, French fries, or vegetable crudités for dipping.

**2 cups raw cashews, soaked in hot water for 15 minutes, then rinsed and drained**

**3 tablespoons vegetable oil**

**2 garlic cloves, peeled**

**2 tablespoons nutritional yeast**

**1 teaspoon miso paste**

**2 teaspoons salt**

**½ teaspoon xanthan gum (optional)**

**¾ cup plus 3 tablespoons water (used all at once)**

**1 cup dry white wine**

1. In a high-speed blender or food processor, blend together the cashews, oil, garlic, nutritional yeast, miso paste, salt, xanthan gum (if using), and water, scraping down the sides.

2. Transfer to a medium saucepan, add the wine, and cook over medium heat, whisking occasionally, until the alcohol evaporates and the fondue is warmed through, about 10 minutes. Add more water, if necessary, to reach the desired consistency.

Ingredient Tip: **Miso paste is made from fermented soybeans and is savory with a rich umami flavor. Miso paste adds amazing flavor to tofu, ramen, and other foods and has probiotics to help you keep your gut healthy.**

# Country Gravy

EGG-FREE, FAMILY-FRIENDLY, MAKE-AHEAD, VEGAN
MAKES 1 CUP / PREP TIME: 5 MINUTES

This rich gravy is as easy to love as it is to prepare. Sometimes I like to add a splash of dry white wine to the gravy. The best way to avoid any lumps in your gravy is to sift the flour over the skillet. The gravy can be kept refrigerated in a resealable container for up to 1 week.

**1 tablespoon olive oil or melted homemade Butter or store-bought dairy-free butter**

**1 tablespoon all-purpose flour**

**⅔ cup homemade Cashew Milk or store-bought dairy-free cashew milk**

**1 thyme sprig**

**¼ teaspoon paprika**

**Salt**

**Freshly ground black pepper**

In a small saucepan, heat the oil over medium heat and sift in the flour; whisk until smooth. Gradually whisk in the milk, thyme, and paprika; season with salt and pepper. Bring to a boil and cook, whisking, until thickened, about 2 minutes.

Substitution Tip: Did you roast a chicken or turkey? Use 1 tablespoon of pan drippings in place of the butter or oil for more flavor.

# Egg-Free Mayonnaise

**EGG-FREE, GLUTEN-FREE, MAKE-AHEAD, VEGAN**
MAKES 2 CUPS / PREP TIME: 5 MINUTES, PLUS 1–2 HOURS TO SOAK THE ALMONDS

Almonds are the base of this eggless mayo, which yields a nice balance of acidity and saltiness. This mayonnaise can be refrigerated in a resealable container for up to 1 week.

1 cup blanched almonds, soaked for 1 to 2 hours, rinsed and drained

1 cup neutral-flavored oil

1 tablespoon distilled white vinegar

2 teaspoons sugar

2 teaspoons salt

¾ cup water

In a high-speed blender, blend together the almonds, oil, vinegar, sugar, salt, and water until smooth.

Substitution Tip: For some heat, stir in hot sauce, wasabi, or chopped chipotle peppers in adobo sauce to taste. You can also add garlic and a small amount of powdered mustard for a deeper taste similar to an aioli.

# Creamy Poppy Seed Vinaigrette

FAMILY-FRIENDLY, MAKE-AHEAD, NUT-FREE
MAKES 1 CUP / PREP TIME: 5 MINUTES

Drizzle this slightly sweet, creamy dressing over greens or even cantaloupe. The dressing will keep refrigerated in a resealable container for up to 3 days.

**1 shallot, finely chopped**

**2 tablespoons Egg-Free Mayonnaise or store-bought mayonnaise**

**2 tablespoons sherry vinegar**

**2 teaspoons poppy seeds**

**1 teaspoon Dijon mustard**

**1 teaspoon honey**

**⅓ cup neutral-flavored oil**

**Salt**

**Freshly ground black pepper**

In a small bowl, whisk together the shallot, mayonnaise, vinegar, poppy seeds, mustard, and honey. Slowly whisk in the oil. If it seems too thick, add water, 1 tablespoon at a time, until your reach your preferred consistency; season with salt and pepper and refrigerate.

# Ranch Dressing

EGG-FREE, FAMILY-FRIENDLY, GLUTEN-FREE, MAKE-AHEAD, VEGAN
MAKES 2 CUPS / PREP TIME: 10 MINUTES, PLUS 15 MINUTES TO SOAK CASHEWS

I keep this salad dressing stocked in the fridge for a fast fix on greens and to drizzle over steamed broccoli or grilled veggies. The dressing can be kept refrigerated in a resealable container for up to 1 week.

2 cups raw cashews, soaked in hot water for 15 minutes, then rinsed and drained

¼ cup neutral-flavored oil

¼ cup white wine vinegar

2 teaspoons dried herb blend, such as Italian

1 tablespoon garlic salt

1 teaspoon onion powder

½ teaspoon pepper

1 teaspoon honey

1 cup water

Blend the cashews, oil, vinegar, dried herbs, garlic salt, onion powder, pepper, honey, and water in a blender or food processor until smooth; transfer to a bowl and refrigerate until cold.

# Caesar Parmesan Dressing

FAMILY-FRIENDLY, MAKE-AHEAD
MAKES 1½ CUPS / PREP TIME: 5 MINUTES

I've swapped in mayonnaise in place of the traditional raw egg yolk used in Caesar dressing recipes. I left in anchovy fillet, the other classic ingredient, which gives the dressing the salty umami flavor I remember growing up with, but you can definitely leave it out with little compromise. The dressing can be kept refrigerated in a resealable container for up to 1 week.

1 cup Egg-Free Mayonnaise or store-bought mayonnaise

⅓ cup homemade Grated Parmesan or store-bought dairy-free grated Parmesan

1 tablespoon white wine vinegar

1 tablespoon fresh lemon juice

1½ teaspoons Dijon mustard

1 large anchovy fillet (optional)

Dash Worcestershire sauce

1 garlic clove

½ cup olive oil

Salt

Freshly ground black pepper

In a blender, combine the mayonnaise, Parmesan, vinegar, lemon juice, mustard, anchovy (if using), Worcestershire sauce, and garlic until smooth. With the machine on, slowly stream in the olive oil. If it seems too thick, add water, 1 tablespoon at a time; season with salt and pepper and refrigerate.

Ingredient Tip: **Caesar dressing is for more than just salads. For a spin on roasted or grilled vegetables, try brushing some Caesar dressing on raw broccoli or other vegetables and roast at 400°F for 20 minutes or grill over medium heat for 7 to 8 minutes.**

# Sour Cream & Chive Dressing

FAMILY-FRIENDLY, GLUTEN-FREE, MAKE-AHEAD
MAKES 1 CUP / PREP TIME: 5 MINUTES

This dressing always reminds me of one of my favorite potato chip flavors, sour cream and onion. Besides a green salad, I love using the dressing in a cold or warm potato salad or on top of a baked potato. The dressing can be kept refrigerated in a resealable container for up to 1 week.

½ cup homemade Sour Cream or store-bought dairy-free sour cream

2 tablespoons Egg-Free Mayonnaise or store-bought mayonnaise

2 tablespoons lemon juice

1 tablespoon chopped fresh chives

1 garlic clove, finely chopped

Salt

Freshly ground black pepper

In a small bowl, whisk together the sour cream, mayonnaise, lemon juice, chives, and garlic. If it seems too thick, add water, 1 tablespoon at a time; season with salt and pepper and refrigerate.

Cooking Tip: Dressing consistency depends on how you're using it. Add less water to the dressing if you want it thick and rich and more water if you're using the dressing to coat potato salad. To make this dressing an onion dip perfect for potato chips and raw veggies, finely chop 1 cup of sweet yellow onion and cook over medium-high heat in 1 teaspoon of oil until caramelized, about 8 to 10 minutes. Season with salt and pepper and let the onions cool slightly before mixing it in with the sour cream and chive mixture.

Printed in Great Britain
by Amazon